D0989842

ONE HUNDRED YEARS *of* WISCONSIN FORESTRY

1904 – 2004

©2004 Wisconsin Woodland Owners Association Inc.

All rights reserved. No part of this publication may be reproduced or transmitted in any form or by any means,
electronic or mechanical, including photocopying and recording, or by any information storage
or retrieval system without permission in writing from the publisher.

Library of Congress Catalog Card Number: 2004107264
ISBN: 1-931599-17-3

09 08 07 06 05 04   6 5 4 3 2 1

Contributing Editors: Randall Rohe, Stephen Miller, Tim Eisele
Project Manager: Becky Peck
Creative Director: Kathie Campbell
Graphic Designers: Colin Harrington and Todd Garrett

Printed on recycled Wisconsin paper by Worzalla of Stevens Point, Wisconsin.

Trails Custom Publishing, a division of Trails Media Group Inc.
P.O. Box 317, Black Earth, WI 53515
(800) 236-8088 www.trailscustompublishing.com

This book is dedicated to the professional foresters of Wisconsin—past, present, and future.
Through their hard work and application of sustainable forestry practices, the forests of our state
have recovered from near ruin and continue to increase and thrive today. As Wisconsin moves into the next 100 years,
Wisconsin forests will remain abundant and productive for future generations.

CONTENTS

WISCONSIN'S GOVERNOR JIM DOYLE declared 2004 "The Year of Wisconsin Forestry" to commemorate the 100th anniversary of the appointment of the first chief state forester of Wisconsin—E. M. Griffith, in 1904—and to celebrate the contributions of forestry professionals and forestry organizations in our state throughout the last century. This book tells the story of the evolution of sustainable forestry in Wisconsin following the devastation of our forests during the late nineteenth and early twentieth centuries, when most of Wisconsin's vast forest resource was cleared to help build the great cities of the Midwest and to promote agriculture.

Since that time, starting with the Wisconsin legislature's recognition that our forests needed to be brought back and protected, our knowledge of the ecological, social, and economic value of our forests has grown, as has our knowledge of how to manage these forests sustainably to provide multiple benefits now and for future generations.

This is a story about the land—the history of forest science, fire-fighting technology, and public policy. It is an account of bold individuals who were ahead of their time, plain folk whose creativity led to new discoveries, and countless hard-working citizens and professionals. Because of this journey, trees once again cover nearly half of our state, and the acres of forest and number of trees within the forest continue to grow.

Wisconsin forests are at the core of the history of this state. Wisconsin would not be what it is today without our forests, and our forests would not be here without the dedicated efforts of the individuals and organizations that are profiled in these pages. Increasingly, society lacks a close relationship with the land and neither acknowledges nor appreciates the bounty of blessings that we receive from our natural resources. Our forests provide clean air and water, habitat for wildlife, recreation, spiritual renewal, and more than 5,000 products that we depend on daily. We hope that this book will bring the history of Wisconsin forests alive for the reader and bring home the message that sustainable forestry benefits every Wisconsin citizen.

Paul DeLong, Chief State Forester, Department of Natural Resources, Division of Forestry

Alvin L. Barden, President, Wisconsin Woodland Owners Association Inc.

One Hundred Years of Wisconsin Forestry is the result of the hard work of many people.
Special acknowledgment is given to the Wisconsin Woodland Owners Association, whose dedication to publishing this book
brings the story of Wisconsin forestry alive for current and future generations; contributing editors Randall E. Rohe, Stephen Miller,
and Tim Eisele; and the Department of Natural Resources Division of Forestry for technical assistance.

"UPON THE RIVERS *which are tributary to the Mississippi, and also upon those which empty themselves in Lake Michigan, there are interminable forests of pine, sufficient to supply all the wants of the citizens in the country, from which this supply can be drawn for all time to come."*

—Wisconsin Congressman Ben C. Eastman, 1852

Congressman Eastman's optimism proved premature. Fifty years after he spoke, the boom in lumbering reduced the state's great woodlands to shadows of their former magnificence. Virgin stands fell to ax and saw, satisfying America's thirst for wood for building homes, factories, bridges, and railroads. What remained was cutover land, stumps, and unrealistic visions of turning northern Wisconsin into rich farms.

After the lumbering era, the road began toward a profession of forestry that worked in concert with nature to create the Wisconsin of today, a land once again covered by forests. The journey was one of debates, arguments, false starts, and competing interests. But what emerged is the state's reputation today as an international leader in forestry. One hundred years of effort have produced sustainable forests—providing employment, wood products, solitude, beauty, wildlife habitat, recreation, preservation of soil, cleaner air, and clearer streams and lakes.

How far has Wisconsin come? The state has more forest now than any time since inventories began in 1936. Almost 50 percent of Wisconsin is covered by trees, and acreage is actually increasing.

Forests contribute to the economic, ecological, and cultural health of our state.

THE EVER-CHANGING FOREST [1]

During the past century, tree species in the North Woods changed with logging, agriculture, and fire. However, little was known about the ancient forests in northern Wisconsin until recently. In the mud of a few lakes and bogs lies a 10,000-year record. The seeds, charcoal, and pollen that each forest produced are preserved in ooze.

Albert Swain, of the Center for Climatic Research, University of Wisconsin, has looked at changes at Hell's Kitchen Lake, a small kettle lake in northern Wisconsin. Trees that generally dominate mature forest here include hemlock, sugar maple, and yellow birch. When there is no fire, these species tend to replace white pine, red pine, aspen, and paper birch, although replacement of white pine is slow because of its long life span. The average interval between fires during the first 1,000 years of record was 100 years, and during the second 1,000 years it

| HEMLOCK | ALDER | RED PINE | WHITE CEDAR | WHITE PINE | ASPEN | YELLOW BIRCH | WHITE PINE | OAK |

100–300 AD

was 140 years. Most likely this accounts for the abundance of hemlock and yellow birch between 1,200 and 120 years ago.

Longer intervals between fires, particularly during the past 600 years, may have resulted from a relatively moister climate. White pine prevailed twice in the past 2,000 years, along with yellow birch and hemlock from about 25 BC to 275 AD and again from 1378 to 1858. Fires were less common then, and white pine flourished during times of plentiful rainfall.

On the other hand, forests around Hell's Kitchen Lake 1,200 years ago were aspen and paper birch, similar to today. No increase of white pine and hemlock followed the birch increase of 120 years ago. Most likely this reflects a response to the earliest logging and clearing along river corridors, followed by fires, which eliminated many potential sources of seed.

HEMLOCK   WHITE CEDAR   ALDER   YELLOW BIRCH   WHITE PINE   OAK   RED PINE   JACK PINE

1300—1500 AD

CHAPTER ONE

THE RISE AND FALL OF LUMBERING (PRE-1904)
WISCONSIN FORESTS ARE DEVASTATED

Forests change in response to natural events and human activities. In southern Wisconsin, before European settlement, from 1825 to 1880, fire was the most significant disturbance. Farther north, the chief factor was wind. Before the arrival of Europeans, forests blanketed most of Wisconsin.[1]

EARLY WISCONSIN

Prior to Euramerican settlement, mixed hardwood and conifer forest covered the major portion of northern Wisconsin. The hardwoods were mainly hard maple, yellow birch, basswood, American elm, rock elm, and red oak. Beech occurred only along Lake Michigan and Green Bay. Hemlock was the principal conifer associated with hardwoods, but the forest contained scattered areas of white pine, balsam fir, and white spruce as well. Within this mixed hardwood and conifer forest were lowland or swamp areas characterized by white cedar, black spruce, tamarack, balsam, black ash, and elm. Sandy soils in parts of central and northern Wisconsin supported white pine, red pine, jack pine, and scrub oak. Oak, hickory, hard maple, basswood, black walnut, and white ash dominated the southern forest, which also contained extensive prairie openings covered with thick grasses and interspersed with hardwood islands.[2]

NATIVE AMERICAN INFLUENCES

A romantic notion is the forest primeval, a continuous, closed-canopy landscape of huge trees. Many believe the first Europeans to reach Wisconsin found an unbroken virgin forest. They assume that interference with natural succession began with white settlement. In reality, Native Americans greatly influenced the vegetation of Wisconsin, and much of what the first Europeans saw was the result of their actions.

Native Americans affected the forest by

An impressive stand of red pine. Very few trees like these survived Wisconsin's lumbering era.

In 1872, about 35 miles north of Shawano, lumbermen cut a white pine with a diameter that measured over six feet at the base and 43 inches at 70 feet. Attaining the largest size of any tree in the state and prized for quality and its workability, white pine was the ideal wood for all building purposes and could be easily transported by water, the major form of log transportation.

clearing trees for village sites, campsites, agricultural fields, and other purposes. They changed the forests by use of fire; through gathering plants for food, drugs, fiber, and other uses; through accidental and intentional introduction of plants; and by their influence on the population of large mammals.[3]

John Curtis, author of *Wisconsin Vegetation*, estimated that Native Americans affected 47–50 percent of the vegetation cover of the state. Native Americans had the greatest impact on fire-susceptible communities such as savanna, grassland, and pine forests.[4]

THE LUMBERING DAYS

Euramerican settlement had relatively little impact on the forests of most of Wisconsin until the lumbering era. While the first sawmill in Wisconsin may have been built as early as 1809, little lumbering occurred until the cessions of Indian lands in 1836, and real development came after the Civil War. By 1869, lumber production had reached more than one billion board feet of lumber, and Wisconsin occupied fourth place among the lumber-producing states of the Union.[5]

Pulpwood production in Wisconsin began in 1871 when an Appleton paper mill began using ground wood pulp from aspen. Previously, the

THE LUMBERING ERA[1]

Few images more graphically illustrate the destruction wrought by lumbering than this photo of a log drive on the Clam River in northwestern Wisconsin. Large logs choke the entire stream, and in the background is a cutover landscape with only a few survivors of forest still standing.

Historians often divide the Wisconsin lumbering era into three distinct phases, separated by periods of transition in which methods and technology of one phase overlap with another.

WHITE PINE/RIVER DRIVE PHASE

This phase lasted from the beginning of the lumbering era to about 1890. During this period, white pine was the major species harvested, and waterways transported logs to the mills. A series of nearly snowless winters, the exhaustion of pine near drivable streams, and the increasing use of hemlock and hardwoods that waterlogged and sank in the streams initiated the beginning of the next phase.

HARDWOOD/RAIL PHASE

This phase extended from about 1890 to 1920. Logs reached mills mainly by railroad because of the depletion of white pine near rivers. The primary trees were hardwoods such as oak, maple, birch, and elm. During the early years of the lumbering era, there were many small operators. By the 1890s, however, the emphasis was on large numbers. Huge sawmills, high production, vast acreages of timber, and large-scale operations were the trend until the 1920s.

PULPWOOD/ROAD PHASE

After World War I, with large holdings of hardwoods cut, emphasis shifted to smaller-scale operations and fuller utilization of timber and timber varieties. Trucks and Caterpillar tractors replaced the logging railroad. The logging camp gradually disappeared, and small, portable and semiportable sawmills became common. Pulpwood—such as aspen, fir, and spruce—for paper mills, ties, posts, and poles largely replaced saw logs.

7

This sawmill, located in the small northeastern Chippewa County community of Ruby, produced as much as 2.5 million feet of lumber, mostly hardwoods, annually. The sawmill burned in 1915, and soon afterward, Ruby became one of the many ghost towns left in the wake of the lumbering era.

state's paper mills had utilized rags, straw, and other materials. Thereafter, the pulp and paper industry expanded as the use of wood pulp spread. The northern forests became an important source of raw material. Mills were built along the Wisconsin, Chippewa, Flambeau, Fox, and other rivers in the northern two-thirds of the state. Spruce supplied most of the pulp at first. Meanwhile, lumber output rapidly increased until reaching peak production in 1892, when mills cut 4.1 billion feet, more than triple what had been cut two decades earlier.[6]

Throughout the nineteenth and early twentieth centuries, both the federal and state governments followed policies that favored widespread and intensive logging to clear the land and provide roads and other infrastructure that would lead to a permanent agricultural economy. Wood was shipped to Chicago and to the East. Wisconsin's lumber helped build the nation. The forests appeared so vast that few people thought the resource could be exhausted. While lumbermen cut, neither the U.S. Congress nor the state legislature drew on their authority to any material effect to maintain the self-renewing productivity of timberlands. Indeed, mostly they did nothing on behalf of forests.[7]

Federal policy severely limited Wisconsin's

ability to protect the forests' sustainability. Moreover, forestry had not yet emerged as a profession in the United States, and many believed farming would follow logging.[8]

AN EARLY WARNING

But voices of caution began to be heard. In 1897, Filibert Roth, a German-born special forestry agent of the U.S. Department of Agriculture who conducted a survey of Wisconsin forests, warned that of the original stand of 130 billion feet of pine, only about 17 billion remained. In addition, the state still possessed 12 billion feet of hemlock and 16 billion feet of various hardwoods. All this totaled only 45 billion feet—barely enough to maintain the industry for a decade at the current rate of production.[9]

ONE THOUSAND SAWMILLS

Yet the cutting continued, and between 1899 and 1904, Wisconsin led the nation in lumber production. During the years of its dominance, the lumber industry affected nearly every aspect of the state's economy. Almost every city located north of a line drawn from Fond du Lac to La Crosse began as a lumber town. Lumbering improved and expanded transportation

facilities. It cleared lands for agriculture. It gave employment to settlers and provided a market for agricultural products. It brought money as well as people from other areas and helped populate the state. It fostered the establishment of many secondary industries that used wood as a raw material. In 1890 alone, lumbering in Wisconsin supported 1,000 sawmills that employed more than 55,000 men in the woods and mills. That year the industry paid more than $15 million in wages and produced goods worth more than $35 million. At the industry's peak, the value of the lumber produced approached $70 million annually or more than the average annual production of gold in the entire United States.[10]

END OF AN ERA

After 1904, Wisconsin's lumber production steadily declined, although the state still ranked among the five largest lumber producers for another five years. In 1920, Wisconsin ranked 10th in U.S. lumber production. In 1929, it had dropped to 14th place. From 1920 to 1930, the annual cut totaled less than one billion board feet. In 1930, lumbering ranked only 14th among the state's industries, and Wisconsin no longer held an important position among the leading lumber producers of the nation.

At this time, however, pulpwood production was becoming the state's leading forest industry. From 1899 to 1929, while lumber production plummeted, pulpwood consumption experienced a 560 percent gain. The cutting of the last large stands of virgin hardwood in the 1930s marked the end of the lumbering era.[11]

Near the close of the nineteenth century, Roth described the effects of lumbering on the forests of northern Wisconsin. In 40 years, he noted, the lumber companies had logged nearly the entire northern portion of the state. The pine had disappeared from most of the mixed forest, and the greater part of the pinery itself had been cut. Exotic species (such as quack grass, Kentucky bluegrass, and thistle) introduced during logging operations became established in some openings and have persisted for more than a century. Also, fires followed most logging operations and considerably altered the forest. These fires burned nearly half of northern Wisconsin at least once. In 1898, Roth described about three million acres as without any forest cover and several million more as covered only by the dead and dying remnants of the former forest. In many of the pine areas, the repeated fires left large tracts of bare wastes or stump prairies, covered only

THE PESHTIGO FIRE [2]

The Peshtigo Fire not only stripped the land of all trees, but also burned their roots and left holes up to 70 feet wide that pocked the landscape. It burned the soil to a depth of two to three feet in places and left nothing but sand and ashes. The fire had a devastating effect on wildlife, killing thousands of deer and other animals.

In the history of the United States, one forest fire stands alone as the most calamitous. While the fire ravaged parts of six counties in northeastern Wisconsin, the greatest devastation occurred in the town of Peshtigo. A comparatively snowless winter and an unprecedented summer drought in 1871 left northern Wisconsin parched and tinder dry. Many small, human-caused fires burned sporadically. Eventually the fires spread. On the night of October 8, a thunderous roar aroused the people of Peshtigo, a lumber town of 1,700 residents. The sky was ablaze and the air filled with thick, choking smoke.

Many accounts describe tornado-like winds and "great sheets of fire falling on the land." The fire spread so rapidly that within four hours it burned an area 40 miles long and 10 miles wide along the western shore of Green Bay. The scene after gave evidence of the fire's intensity. Fire consumed not only trees but also their roots and left deep cavities in the ground.

In all the fire took the lives of 1,200–1,300 people—five or six times as many as the Chicago Fire, which occurred the same day. Seven thousand people were left destitute.

with weeds, grasses, and a few scattered scrub oak, aspen, or birch. Logging and fire reduced spruce-tamarack swamps to open muskeg or sedge.[12]

DEVASTATING FIRES

The logging methods of the time were an invitation to fire. The loggers removed only the choicest pine, leaving on the forest floor great heaps of branches and tops known as "slashings." One spark could start a fire, which would not only burn the forest but also damage the soil and reduce its productivity. These fires transformed acres upon acres into barren wastes of blackened stumps, many of which are still visible today.[13]

The lack of organized fire protection permitted fires to burn practically at will and caused widespread devastation. Unless the forest fires threatened life or property, the public showed little concern. Many still believed that the forests were inexhaustible and that forest fires stimulated agricultural development.

One or more fires swept through the slashings on most of the lumbered areas. The Peshtigo Fire of October 1871 burned more than 1.25 million acres in northeastern Wisconsin; the Comstock Fire of May 1891 burned 64,000 acres

The white pine is the largest and one of the longest-living trees of the forest. Ultimate heights of over 200 feet are common and ages of 400 years or more are possible. In the old-growth northern hardwood forests, white pine occurred singly or in groves towering above the hardwood canopy.

LUMBER PRODUCTION IN WISCONSIN

While Wisconsin achieved regional importance in the 1840s as a lumber producer, the large volume of logging did not begin until after the Civil War. Rapid expansion of railroads westward and the settlement of the nearly treeless Great Plains precipitated an enormous increase in lumber production. Lumber production was usually recorded in board feet. One board foot is 12 inches by 12 inches by 1 inch thick.

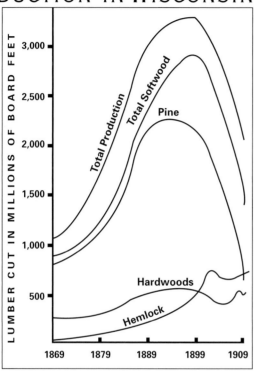

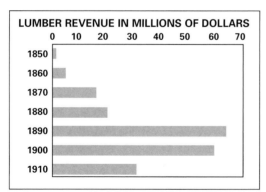

in Barron County; and the Phillips Fire of July 1894 burned some one million acres in Price County.[14]

NEW LANDSCAPES

The combination of fire-degraded soil and a lack of pioneer conifers, such as red and white pine, meant the forests that existed following lumbering were very different. A striking feature of the postlumbering forest was the great increase of aspen and jack pine. The almost entire disappearance of white pine and the great reduction of northern hardwoods were also notable. Within the forest, upland openings of braky grasslands were often common.[15]

The changes in vegetation caused by logging and the fires that followed greatly affected wildlife populations, exemplified by the white-tailed deer. Prior to 1800, deer were largely concentrated in the prairie-oak and maple forest areas of southern Wisconsin. The mature forest of the north was only secondary range.[16]

The ax and plow removed the features of southern Wisconsin that had attracted and held deer, but in the north the ax and saw improved the range. Opening the forest floor to sunlight by ax and fire fostered a growth of plants, which

formed superb food and cover for deer. Deer that were once most abundant in southern Wisconsin moved north into acres of young forest that followed logging. Their range expanded to the shore of Lake Superior, where they had rarely been seen before. Sometime before 1900, expanding deer habitat caused an early population peak. A combination of market hunting and uncontrolled forest fires resulted in a population decline after 1900 that probably reached a low around 1910.[17]

CHANGES IN THE SOUTH

While logging and the fires that followed almost completely changed the forest of northern Wisconsin, agriculture greatly altered the forests, prairies, and savannas of southern Wisconsin. More than any other Wisconsin plant community, the prairie has been subject to direct destruction for agricultural purposes. Prairies once covered about two million acres of Wisconsin. Now probably no more than several thousand acres survive. The great majority of the southern lowland conifer swamp has been drained and converted to farmland. Especially in the late 1800s, many tamarack swamps were cut over and converted to mowing meadows or pastures. At the same time, the cessation of Native American fires caused an increase (about 40 percent) in the acreage of oak-hickory forest, especially in the rougher sections of the savanna, which proved unsuitable for agriculture.[18]

DREAM FARMS

In many parts of the United States, the plow had followed the ax, and many people expected the same thing to happen in Wisconsin. As William A. Henry, dean of the University of Wisconsin College of Agriculture, noted: "Northern Wisconsin will not revert to a wilderness with the passing of the lumber, but will be occupied by a thrifty class of farmers."[19] The effort to encourage settlement of the Cutover began before the turn of the century. Many envisioned northern Wisconsin as a vast new agricultural frontier once lumbering ended; some even dreamed of a second dairy empire. Although it never happened, it was not from lack of effort. Lumber and land companies, county and state governments, and even the University of Wisconsin–Extension promoted the development of agriculture in the north. Hyperbole-filled brochures identified northern Wisconsin as "the great cheese section," "the land of the big red clover," or "the hay and potato belt."[20]

After widespread pine logging, some forest had begun to regenerate, but many pine areas lacked seed trees and repeated fires had eliminated reproduction, consumed organic matter, and degraded the soil. These conditions favored open areas of brush, grass, and sedges (i.e."stump prairies") and the establishment of species such as aspen, white birch, and cherry. This stump prairie is located west of Langlade in Langlade County.

13

For several decades many assumed that pine stumps were the most serious obstacle to converting the Cutover into farmland. The UW College of Agriculture, the U.S. Department of Agriculture, and private agencies worked to find quick, cheap, easy ways to remove stumps—a task they never accomplished. Yet in his handbook, William Henry wrote, "The general absence of the 'Heart Root' in the timber of Northern Wisconsin renders stump pulling less difficult than is generally supposed. The owner of this farm, located in Taylor County, began with small means several years ago. By his labor alone he has acquired a property that insures him independence through life and an inheritance of some consequence for his children."

A disproportionately large number of settlers who tried to farm the Cutover were European immigrants. They came to this area because other (better) lands farther south had already been settled. Many of these people had found limited economic opportunity in mining and factory work or were peasants who arrived directly from Europe. The Peter Legacy family, French-Canadian immigrants, is shown at its farm near Washburn in 1895.

AN 1890 EXODUS

In 1890, nearly a quarter million of Wisconsin's population migrated to Minnesota, Iowa, Nebraska, Kansas, and the Dakotas. At that time, the 29 northern counties had only 361,500 people, fully one-third of them foreign born. Unless "farms followed stumps," the northern counties faced a decrease in population, industry, and even railroads as lumbering neared its peak, and one lumber company after another exhausted its timber, closed its sawmills, and moved on to other regions.[21]

To counter the migration to other states and to attract new people to Wisconsin, the state established a Board of Immigration in 1895 and located a secretary at Rhinelander. In the same year, William A. Henry published *Northern Wisconsin, A Handbook for the Home Seeker.* It was lavishly illustrated with photos, and within a year some 50,000 copies had been distributed to prospective settlers. This vigorous immigration policy was responsible in part for the three million acres of land brought into farms between 1890 and 1900. Faculty members at the University of Wisconsin and the UW–Extension did intensive studies of the region and produced analyses of the northern economy and handbooks for new settlers;

A professor of botany and agriculture and manager of the University of Wisconsin farm, William A. Henry was instrumental in establishing the agricultural experimental station at the UW in 1883 and the first farmers' institutes and agricultural short-course programs in the United States in 1885. He worked effectively to secure support for an agricultural college within the university and became the first dean of the College of Agriculture in 1891.

The caption for this photo, which appeared in Henry's *Handbook for the Homeseeker*, told prospective settlers that it was a view of Edward Dascam's 64-acre oat field near Antigo in 1895. "During the summer of 1894 and winter of 1895 Mr. Dascam cleared this land of its heavy timber, selling from the tract logs and wood sufficient to pay for clearing the land, fencing, plowing among the stumps with a shovel plow, sowing and dragging in the oats. . . . The enormous crop of oats which stood from five to six feet high over the whole tract . . . gives one a good idea of the natural fertility of the land and shows how productive it is even when the green timber has just been removed." History showed, however, that this type of agricultural success was not the common experience.

Writers have delineated the boundaries of the Cutover in a number of different ways. Robert Gough, author of *Farming the Cutover*, has it corresponding closely to the Northern Highlands, a physiographic division. The 18 counties that he includes in the region were the least developed in 1900; grew the fastest between 1900 and 1940; lost farmland, with one exception, at a higher rate than the state average between 1940 and 1990; and whose residents shared a communal historical experience.

experimented with early maturing soybeans, peas, and corn; attempted to adapt new crops such as sunflowers for silage; refined dairy techniques for northern uses; and developed methods for removing pine stumps.[22]

A number of conditions encouraged agricultural settlement of the Cutover. Because most lumber companies had no interest in dealing in Cutover lands, many allowed them to revert to the government for taxes or sold them for a few cents an acre. Most of the prairies of the Midwest had been settled by the end of the nineteenth century, and the Cutover was the only large area of cheap land open to settlement.[23]

While lumbering continued, a ready market existed for farm products. The logging roads and railroads provided a means of transportation, and lumbering offered the farmers a means to supplement their income during the winter. Yet the thin, rocky soils and short growing season made much of northern Wisconsin ultimately unsuited for agriculture. In 1898, Filibert Roth described only 22.5 percent of the land of 27 northern counties as good agricultural land, 40.3 percent as of medium value, and 37.2 percent as suitable only for forests. Unfortunately, most people did not pay attention to his report.[24]

EARLY CONSERVATION

Many people regard the nineteenth century as a period of unbridled exploitation of the state's natural resources—especially its forests—with little concern for the results. The beginnings of the conservation movement and with it the early development of forestry, however, occurred during the lumbering era. In 1855, in the *Transactions of the State Agricultural Society*, Increase Lapham made a plea for forest conservation. Trees, he explained, maintained the balance of nature by preserving moisture in the soil, regulating stream flow, providing nutrients for the soil, and restoring oxygen to the air.[25]

The Wisconsin Commissions of School and University Lands (later the Commissioners of Public Lands) in 1860 began to hire forest rangers during the logging season to protect the lands under its jurisdiction from timber trespass. Through a series of federal land grants between 1838 and 1866, Wisconsin came into possession of millions of acres of land. The state constitution committed administration of these lands to the Wisconsin Commissions of School and University Lands, which consisted of the secretary of state, state treasurer, and attorney general.[26]

In 1867, the state legislature created a special Conservation Commission to investigate and report on the "injurious effects of clearing land of forests" and "the best method of preventing the evil effects of their destruction."[27] In its report published the same year, the commission called attention to the fact that the forests of southern Wisconsin "no longer yield a supply adequate for the wants of the present inhabitants; and the forest of the northern regions, heretofore considered the inexhaustible storehouse of wood for the adjoining treeless districts, will soon be so reduced that the people must look elsewhere for their supplies."[28]

With remarkable insight for the time, the report stated that "Clearing away the forests diminishes the flow of water from springs, increases the suddenness and magnitude of floods and torrents, washes away the soil, exposes the State and all its inhabitants to the biting and blighting effects of the winds which will sweep over the surface with unabated violence, causes snow to accumulate in drifts, leaving portions bare and unprotected while other portions are buried in accumulated masses of snow and loosens sandy soil so that it will be blown away."[29]

Despite the fact that the state printed and distributed 5,000 copies of the report, no steps were taken to remedy the situation.

Increase Lapham was the state's first scientist and first conservationist. In fact, he might be called our first ecologist, for he was the first person to examine and record the Wisconsin landscape from an ecological viewpoint. Lapham considered the human forces that were rapidly changing the Wisconsin landscape and spoke forcefully of the destruction of Wisconsin forests and the potential effects of deforestation on agriculture and water resources.

"To Increase A. Lapham, the state's first great scientist, belongs the credit of seeing the need of forest conservation a generation in advance of his fellows, and of doing his utmost to direct their attention to the problem." —M. M. Quaife (1921)

17

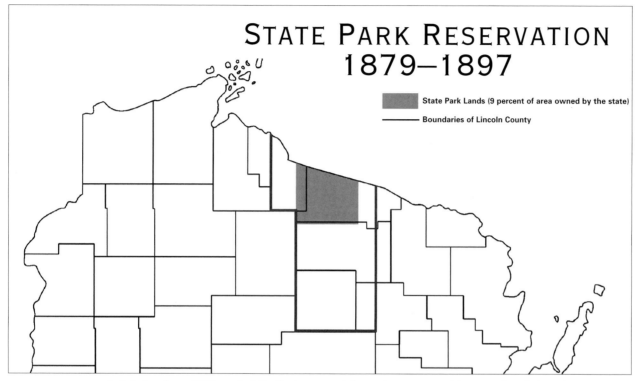

STATE PARK RESERVATION 1879–1897

State Park Lands (9 percent of area owned by the state)

Boundaries of Lincoln County

A state law from 1878 created the first state park (state forest reserve) by reserving timbered tracts owned by the state in several northern townships. Total land reserved was slightly less than 60,000 acres. In 1897, the legislature approved the land's appraisal and sale, which sold for an average of $10.40 per acre.

The devastating Peshtigo Fire of 1871 brought the seriousness of forest fires tragically to the attention of the public. Except for a relief appropriation for seed grain and potatoes for the fire survivors in Oconto, Brown, and Door Counties, the only legislation resulting was a law prohibiting the burning of woods, prairies, or cranberry bogs between August 1 and November 30. While ineffective, due to lack of enforcement, this law did establish the principle of a closed season on burning.[30]

AN 1876 REFORESTATION

In 1876, Walter Ware planted 1,876 trees on his farm near Hancock to celebrate the centennial of American independence. He was probably the first person to practice forestry in Wisconsin. Reforestation on an extensive scale, however, had to await adequate protection from fire. In 1878, the state legislature set aside more than 50,000 acres in 24 separate townships in northern Wisconsin as a state forest reserve to protect the headwaters of certain streams that drain into the Mississippi River. In 1880, it made a similar withdrawal of land at the headwaters of the Chippewa River for the same purpose. Unfortunately, these actions proved temporary.[31]

Walter Ware began reforesting an old agricultural field near Hancock in 1869 with white and red pine seedlings that he obtained from the margins of the Leola Marsh. Ware completed the planting in 1876 as his own way to celebrate the centennial of the United States's Declaration of Independence.

In 1961, Floyd Foster, with assistance from the Wisconsin Conservation Department, completed a combination timber harvest–forest stand improvement cut of the Ware plantation. The cut took over 25,000 board feet of saw logs from seven acres of land.

AN EARLY ATTEMPT
AT SELECTIVE CUTTING

In 1889, Charles Pollack acquired a tract of timberland near Merrill and practiced selective cutting —cutting only the mature trees and removing any diseased or otherwise defective trees. Pollack's effort was one of the earliest attempts at selective cutting by a private landowner. The existing tax structure and lack of adequate fire protection, however, made more and larger such undertakings unfeasible.

Andrew Merryman, a prominent Marinette lumberman, thought much of northern Wisconsin was better suited to growing trees than crops, most likely based on his experience growing up on a hard-scrabble farm in Maine. In 1894, he went to Maine and obtained spruce seed cones to plant on some of his Cutover land in Marinette County. He hoped to eventually cut the spruce for pulp for the region's growing number of paper mills. Forest fires, however, doomed his experiment to failure.[32]

FIRE WARDENS

In 1895, as a result of the Phillips and other severe fires the preceding year, the state legislature made town supervisors and road superintendents ex officio fire wardens. They had authority to prohibit burning between July and October when conditions warranted, employ firefighters to fight ongoing fires, prevent the setting of fires, post fire warnings, and report the occurrence of fires and the resulting damage. They received $1.50 for each day worked (up to 10 days a year for firefighting and 5 days for posting warnings and enforcing the fire laws). No town, however, could spend more than $100 a year.[33]

This law also provided a penalty for starting a fire and leaving it unextinguished and for burning without a written permit during the closed season. Further, it made the party responsible for starting a fire liable specifically for any damage resulting, and it regulated railroads to reduce the occurrence of fires along their lines. In 1897, the state legislature authorized the state forestry warden to appoint at least one fire warden in each organized township, make rules and regulations for their guidance, and supervise their activities. Town fire wardens received authority to impress firefighters and became responsible for reporting violations of the fire laws to the district attorney, who had specific responsibility to take legal action if the evidence warranted.[34]

AN INVESTIGATION OF
FOREST CONDITIONS

Disturbed by the rapidity of the depletion of the state's timber supply and the number of disastrous fires that occurred annually, the 1897 legislature ordered an investigation of forest conditions and the development of a plan for the protection and management of the state's forest resources. The legislature appropriated no funds, but through the cooperation of the U.S. Department of Agriculture and the State Geological Survey, Filibert Roth, later professor of forestry at the University of Michigan, agreed to survey northern Wisconsin. Based on Roth's findings and other evidence presented, the Forestry Commission recommended the establishment of a State Forestry Department, the organized protection of forest property by the state, the establishment of forest reserves, and provisions for technical assistance to forest landowners. The 1898 legislature failed to pass a bill embodying these recommendations. The 1899 legislature did, however, pass two laws affecting fire control. One restricted the appointment of town fire wardens to certain specified counties unless requested by the local authorities. The other transferred the office and duties of state forestry warden from the Land Commission to the secretary of state. In 1901 the legislature repealed the latter law and made game wardens ex officio fire wardens with authority to take action on fires.[35]

Meanwhile, at the national level, Gifford
Pinchot, the first chief of the U.S. Division of
Forestry (now the U.S. Forest Service) convened
an organizational meeting of the Society of
American Foresters on November 30, 1900. Since
its formation, its primary purpose has been to
advance the profession of forestry in the United
States through publications, standardizing forest
terminology, and setting standards for forestry
education. Through these activities, the organization
has helped advance the practice of forestry
in Wisconsin.[36]

THE FIRST COMPREHENSIVE FORESTRY LAW

Wisconsin enacted its first comprehensive
forestry law in 1903, essentially the same one
recommended by the commission of 1897. On
February 1, 1904, E. M. Griffith, the state's first
professionally trained forester, reported for work
and opened a new chapter in the state's relationship
with its natural resources.[37]

CHAPTER TWO

THE GRIFFITH YEARS (1904–1915)
THE EMERGENCE OF PROFESSIONAL FORESTRY

"THE GENERATION *yet unborn had done nothing for me, and I do not want to sacrifice too much for them.*"

—Senator Timothy O. Howe

"THE DAMAGE *which was ruthlessly committed will require more than a generation to mend, but . . . the strong work of restoration will be generously aided.*"

—Governor J. O. Davidson

Senator Timothy O. Howe's statement probably reflected the thinking of a significant part of the state. Yet the voices of Governor Davidson, E. M. Griffith, and others were heard.

While there had been sporadic attempts to conserve Wisconsin's natural resources before 1900, they proved ineffectual at best, primarily because most people failed to see any pressing or immediate need for such regulation. Indeed, the term *conservation* did not become part of popular usage until 1907, after President Theodore Roosevelt's speech before the National Editorial Association. Before that time the word was *preservation*. President Roosevelt set a precedent, however, by speaking of "the conservation of our natural resources and their proper use as constituting the fundamental problem which underlies almost every other problem of our national life."[1]

FIRSTS FOR FORESTRY

The 1903 legislature passed Wisconsin's first comprehensive forestry law, creating the Department

Fred Wilson poses at the Star Lake Plantation in 1956 after the third thinning of the stand within 42 years. Established in 1913, Star Lake was the state's first plantation.

of State Forestry under the control of the Board of State Forest Commissioners, which consisted of the attorney general, the secretary of state, the state treasurer, and two public members appointed by the governor. This law prohibited the sale of state lands (with the exception of swamplands, farmlands, and woodlots of fewer than 80 acres adjoining farms). The remaining state lands became part of the state forest reserve, which the superintendent of state forests had the responsibility to evaluate.[2]

The Board of State Forest Commissioners had authority to accept grants of land to the state for forestry purposes subject to certification of a clear title by the attorney general. The superintendent of state forests had authority to contract for the sale of fallen timber on state lands, but such contracts required board approval. While the board wished to establish a forest reserve to protect the sources of the state's streams, no existing law authorized such action. The Progressive Party leaders, unable to overcome opposition of the lumber interests to such a plan, finally resorted to selecting 40,000 acres of land and putting it on the open market "at so high a figure that no one would think of buying it." The land returned to the state by default and became the nucleus of the future forest reserve.[3]

Besides setting aside land for a forest reserve, the board's most significant act was appointing a superintendent of forests. Among the tasks delegated to the superintendent were acting as ex officio state forest warden, controlling forest fires, arresting and prosecuting trespassers on state lands, and appointing one or more fire wardens in each town in 28 specified northern counties.[4]

The board appointed E. M. Griffith as Wisconsin's first state forester. Griffith was a technically trained forester who had worked under United States Forestry Division Chief Gifford Pinchot. He had trained at the Sheffield School at Yale and the Biltmore School of Forestry in North Carolina and had practical experience in Germany. He undertook his assignment in 1904 with great dedication and quickly persuaded the board to add another 22,000 acres to the reserve. He then set about bringing the law into harmony with his notions of forestry and acquiring an even larger state timber reserve.[5]

While the 1903 law was a move in the right direction for forestry, many realized more work was needed. In his message to the 1905 legislature, Governor Robert La Follette said, "The state forestry legislation adopted two years ago, defective in many respects, will, it is hoped, be so amended

as to establish this important work upon a permanent and efficient basis." He might have added "and to remove forestry from politics."[6]

LAWS OF 1905

La Follette's support led to the enactment of Chapter 264, Laws of 1905, which changed the title of the superintendent of state forests to state forester and created the State Board of Forestry. This organization was composed predominantly of ex officio members: the president of the university, the dean of the College of Agriculture, the director of the State Geological Survey, the attorney general, and one citizen appointed by the governor.[7]

Most important, the new law added a provision to the statutes requiring that the state forester be a technically trained forester and that he be certified by the secretary of the U.S. Department of Agriculture. Moreover, it altered the duties of the state forester slightly to grant him some discretion in the disposal of state forestlands that were deemed unnecessary for the state forest reserve, and it authorized the forester to maintain forest nurseries, tree plantations, and fire lanes. Further, the State Board of Forestry gained the authority to appoint an assistant state forester (who had to be technically trained in the field) to aid the state

WISCONSIN'S FIRST STATE FORESTER [1]

When E. M. Griffith came to Wisconsin in 1904, he was full of energy and single minded in his devotion to forestry. His sincerity, honesty, and integrity were beyond reproach. Even his enemies agreed that he worked ceaselessly, unselfishly, and devotedly. Indeed, the Wisconsin Supreme Court that had demolished his work in 1915 later went out of its way to pay tribute to Griffith's zeal and honesty.

Wisconsin's first state forester, E. M. Griffith, devoted much time and energy to getting the legislature to pass laws and provide funds for an adequate fire-suppression and fire-fighting system. In this effort, Griffith sought the cooperation of timberland owners, settlers, and railroad companies. His reforestation program included establishment of nurseries first at Trout Lake and then at Tomahawk to provide trees for the reforestation of both state and private lands. He urged the development of farm woodlots and championed a woodlot tax-exemption law, which the legislature passed in 1907. He encouraged a detailed study of forest taxation in Wisconsin, which in final form recommended a severance tax for timberland in place of the annual property tax, thereby postponing the cutting of timber. He worked for the purchase of state forests and parks in the Cutover. He energetically encouraged lumber companies to adopt sound management practices for their timberlands and promoted the improvement of farm woodlands. He even urged the establishment of community forests. In 1908 and 1909, he endorsed a state forest policy and guidelines for tax exemption and tax delinquency of forest-lands. Griffith recommended a portion of the statewide general property tax for forestry. This tax was adopted in 1924. It continues to finance a substantial part of the state's forestry program.

Because only recent emmigrants from continental Europe had any concept of forestry, Griffith tried to educate the public about forestry and its value. He gave numerous lectures about German forestry practices, often illustrated with lantern slides, to community and civic clubs and associations throughout the state. He promoted educational conferences and delivered a series of annual lectures about forestry at the University of Wisconsin. Griffith gave his heart and soul to the development of forestry in Wisconsin, and the state supreme court ruling of 1915 devastated him (see page 36). He left Wisconsin in July 1915 and essentially never worked in forestry again. Ironically, most politicians, newspaper reporters, scientists, and the general public eventually supported his ideas and plans. He was indeed a man ahead of his time.

25

forester in the performance of his duties.[8]

Finally, in an attempt to solve the problem of ever-increasing forest fires, the legislature included a provision in the law allowing the state or an individual whose land was burned through willfulness, malice, or negligence to recover in a civil action double the amount of damages suffered. The forest reserve fund received all money collected by the state under this provision.[9]

The Laws of 1905 increased the annual appropriation for forestry to $9,800, where it remained for six years, and set the state forester's annual salary at $3,000 a year and the assistant's at $1,500. In May 1906, Frank B. Moody, a graduate forester with previous work experience in the Maine woods, became assistant state forester. The Laws of 1905 expanded the forest reserves to include all federal grant lands north of Township 33, which adjoined the northern boundaries of Oconto and Taylor Counties. The State Board of Forestry was to examine and release for sale those lands found to be more valuable for purposes other than forestry.[10]

REFORESTATION FUND ESTABLISHED

In 1906, Senator (previously governor) Robert M. La Follette Sr. secured a grant from Congress of not more than 20,000 acres of unallotted federal lands in the state for forestry purposes, with a reversion clause if the lands were otherwise used. While the secretary of the interior could authorize the sale of scattered or potential agricultural lands, the proceeds had to be used for forest planting. This led to the establishment of the state reforestation fund. The 1907 legislature (Chapter 96, Laws of 1907) authorized the appraisal and sale of all state swampland within Indian reservations to the United States and earmarked the money received for the forest reserve fund. At the same time, it authorized the purchase of tax title lands for inclusion in the forest reserve (Chapter 491, Laws of 1907) and appropriated $10,000 a year for this purpose. In addition, a constitutional amendment was initiated specifically authorizing the state to appropriate money for forestry purposes.[11]

THE BEGINNING OF STATE FORESTS

In 1907, state forests began when Frederick Weyerhaeuser deeded to the state 2,840 acres of land that later became the Brule River State Forest. Subsequent grants from the federal government and purchases from Douglas County and private individuals increased the state forest area to 3,523 acres in 1909.[12]

RESTORATION BECOMES PRIORITY

In May 1908, President Theodore Roosevelt called a conference of state governors at the White House to consider the conservation of the nation's natural resources. Wisconsin Governor J. O. Davidson took an active part in the deliberations of the conference and served on its Resolutions Committee. In an impassioned address, he recounted the history of the national forest destruction and stated, "The damage which was ruthlessly committed will require more than a generation to mend, but it is believed that a thoughtful public interest has been aroused, and the strong work of restoration will be generously aided."[13]

On his return to Wisconsin, Davidson appointed a special State Conservation Commission, headed by Dr. Charles R. Van Hise, president of the University of Wisconsin, to report on conditions in Wisconsin and recommend needed conservation legislation. This commission recommended, among other things, that the state borrow $1 million for the purchase of land needed to consolidate the state forest reserve and that the annual appropriation for the State Board of Forestry be "largely increased."[14]

FIRE-CONTROL MEASURES NEEDED

By 1908, Wisconsin had more than 300 fire wardens in 33 counties, approximately 15 million acres under nominal protection, and a state inspector who checked the condition of locomotives and railroad rights of way to secure compliance with the railroad fire laws and to reduce the number of railroad fires. Yet during 1908, more than 1,400 fires burned nearly 1.25 million acres with an estimated loss of more than $9 million. As a result, timberland owners held a meeting at Eau Claire in November to discuss the situation. Their group (Timber Owners' Association of Wisconsin) appointed a committee of five headed by J. T. Barber of Eau Claire to formulate recommendations.[15]

This committee's report recommended that the state organize fire-protection districts, employ seasonal inspectors and patrolmen to supplement the efforts of the town fire wardens, establish a closed season on burning except by permit, and authorize a tax on timberland of two to two and one-half cents an acre for fire control. The

governor's State Conservation Commission and the Lake States Forestry Conference held at Madison, December 9–10, 1908, endorsed these recommendations. Action taken by the next legislature, however, did little more than authorize the State Board of Forestry to inspect locomotives operating through forest and grass areas and to order railroads to patrol behind trains during dangerously dry times. It was 1911 before the state began to create a comprehensive system of forest-fire protection.[16]

MENOMINEE RESERVATION FORESTS "FINEST IN STATE"

In 1854 the federal government established a reservation for the Menominee Indian tribe 40 miles northwest of Green Bay. A high-quality hardwood and conifer forest covered most of the reservation. The Menominee resisted federal pressure to allot the land to individual tribal members, as had been done on Wisconsin's other Indian reservations, where stands of pine had been cut under federal contract, with no restraints on the logging practices.[17] Griffith later stated in 1906: "It can safely be said that the forests on this reservation are the finest in the state, and . . . gradually forestry regulations should be

introduced in the logging operations and only mature, ripe timber, of which there is an enormous amount, should be cut and the slash piled and burned to prevent forest fires and cuttings so arranged that the growth and reproduction of the most valuable species will be favored."[18]

Just two years later, in response to a 1905 blowdown of 40 million board feet, Senator La Follette vigorously sponsored a bill for the establishment of a logging and milling enterprise on the Menominee Reservation to salvage the storm-damaged timber. In addition, the mill would offer employment to the Indians and at the same time demonstrate the practicality of forestry practice in a logging operation administered by the federal government. La Follette won passage of his Menominee Reservation Bill as the Act of March 28, 1908. It provided for construction of tribal mills and prescribed an allowable annual cut of 20 million board feet of such fully mature and ripened green timber as the U.S. Forest Service should designate, plus any dead or down timber. The act authorized the employment of foresters and other skilled workers as necessary but specifically required the employment of Indians as far as practicable. A sawmill was built at Neopit

Senator La Follette's bill stipulated that only Indians be given logging contracts or employment in the sawmill. The logging operations, however, employed both Indians and non-Indians. In the winter of 1910–1911, five logging camps operated on the Menominee Indian Reservation; two of them had non-Indian foremen. The crew in this photo includes both groups as well.

in 1908, and during 1909 and 1910, selective cutting was done on the Menominee forest with U.S. Department of Agriculture (USDA) Forest Service foresters marking individual trees for harvest in cooperation with the Department of the Interior.

FOREST PRODUCTS LABORATORY ESTABLISHED

Better utilization of Wisconsin's remaining timber supply was an integral component of Griffith's forestry program, and he and his associates vigorously lobbied federal authorities to locate the Forest Products Laboratory (FPL) in Madison. In 1909, the state legislature authorized the regents of the university to spend $50,000 to provide a building for the laboratory. The U.S. Forest Service equipped the lab and paid the salaries of its employees. The FPL began operation in 1910 as a "laboratory of practical research." One of the first problems it tackled was wasteful timber-harvest practices.[19]

VOTERS APPROVE FORESTRY AMENDMENT

The forestry movement incited no violent objection before 1909, and in fact it won some

FOREST PRODUCTS LABORATORY[2]

In 1908, McGarvey Cline, head of a section on wood uses in the U.S. Forest Service, envisioned a centralized "timber testing laboratory." While he initially failed to obtain funds from Congress to build it, he succeeded in obtaining a cooperative agreement with the University of Wisconsin for his lab. Cline then brought together the pioneer wood chemists, engineers, and physicists. It was a unique undertaking, but one that led to fruitful results.

On June 4, 1910, the Forest Products Laboratory (FPL) formally opened with Cline as the director. Scientists from several universities moved to Madison, and the cooperating UW provided a specially constructed laboratory. Initially, the laboratory's research program focused on three areas: determining the physical and chemical properties of the many native species of woods, finding the requirements of various uses in terms of these wood properties, and adapting one to the other as far as possible through scientific manipulation of growth and manufacturing processes.

There were a number of important early successes at the FPL, such as Harry D. Tiemann's humidity-regulated dry kiln. Lumber manufacturers quickly adopted Tiemann's kilns to speed up and control the long and expensive process of drying lumber. The laboratory tested American wood species to acquire a full array of engineering data on them. The wood-using industries utilized this information to select material and species for specific purposes, such as poles, structural timbers, aircraft, boxes, boats, and housing. The FPL's pulp and paper research group studied mechanical as well as chemical pulping at a full-sized experimental ground wood mill at Wausau. Later it developed an entirely new process, semichemical pulping. Chemists at FPL studied the chemical composition of wood, wood distillation and extraction, and the manufacture of ethyl alcohol, glues, wood-preserving chemicals, and chemicals for stabilizing and moisture proofing wood. In the field of wood preservation, the laboratory contributed substantially to the development and standardization of preservatives and treating methods for a range of wood uses in which durability is important. The Forest Products Laboratory played an important role with the U.S. Department of Commerce in standardizing lumber dimensions by assisting the manufacturers, distributors, and consumers of lumber in setting up American standards to replace local and regional standards.

During World Wars I and II and the intervening period, the laboratory's reputation spread around the world, and the FPL became the model for national laboratories in many industrialized and developing countries. By the end of World War II, a growing realization of the pending exhaustion of high-quality timber caused a shift from using lesser-used species to the more efficient use of existing supplies. In 1962, President John F. Kennedy stated, "The Forest Product Laboratory in Madison has returned $70 to the government in taxes for every dollar it has spent in research."

When the U.S. Forest Service established the Forest Products Laboratory in cooperation with the University of Wisconsin in 1910, the concept was that a more rational and economical use of forest products was vital to the material prosperity of the nation. Then, as now, forest conservation involved the protection, management, and cultivation of forest crops, but also the wise utilization of the products harvested from the forest, which has remained the Forest Products Laboratory's main purpose.

Economics was an important objective of conservation. Both Theodore Roosevelt and Gifford Pinchot had stated time and again that forestry was the preservation or conservation of forests by "wise use." As a result, the establishment of the Forest Products Laboratory in Madison represented not only a major advance for forestry in Wisconsin, but also for the nation.

29

During the spring of 1911, a crew under the direction of Frank Moody cleared stumps and plowed an area of 7.5 acres for a nursery at Trout Lake. They completed seeding of the nursery in early July 1911.

By the fall of 1912, an inventory of the Trout Lake nursery showed 933,000 one-year seedlings and 1,299,000 of two-year stock, part of which had already been transplanted. Annual output reached more than one million trees in 1921.

support in the state. In August 1909, on the eve of the first National Conservation Congress, a meeting of individuals and organizations concerned about conservation issues, the *Milwaukee Free Press* announced that "the experience of Wisconsin in the great problem of conserving natural resources will be one of the important contributions to the conference of governors and forestry experts to gather at Washington this week." The *Free Press* boasted that because of the laws passed by the previous two legislatures, Wisconsin ranked third in size of its forest reserves and led all the states of the Northwest in the conservation of natural resources (in 1909, Wisconsin was considered part of the Northwest). Some questions existed as to whether the forest reserves might fall within the classification of works of internal improvement, and thus the state constitution prohibited the use of trust lands or funds for the creation of forest reserves. The legislature of 1907 approved an amendment to permit the state to engage in forestry. Again in 1909, the senate took formal action, but the assembly did not. By joint resolution, however, both houses directed that the amendment be submitted for referendum. In the general election of November 1910, voters approved the amendment by a vote of 62,406 to 45,874.[20]

FORESTRY HEADQUARTERS LOCATES AT TROUT LAKE

During the summer of 1910, Griffith made plans for a forestry headquarters at Trout Lake, northeast of Woodruff. Under the supervision of Assistant State Forester Frank B. Moody, forestry student C. L. Harrington and a crew of three cleared the site for a headquarters building and constructed a firebreak along the edge of the pine stand on Trout Lake. In the early fall, they collected pinecones from treetops at the nearby logging operations of the Yawkey Bissell Lumber Company to plant the following spring. During the 1911 field season, the headquarters buildings at Trout Lake were constructed, the first nursery was established, and 192,000 seedlings purchased from Michigan Agricultural College were planted.[21]

Rangers with small crews and a team of horses reworked old sleigh-haul roads and logging railroad grades and built connecting links to provide 100 miles of wagon roads in the area. During the winter, the first ranger stations, consisting of a dwelling, a barn, and a cabin for laborers, were built. Forester F. G. Wilson drafted the first map to serve for forest protection in anticipation of the four, 55-foot steel lookout towers to be erected the following summer. Ground circuit telephone lines connected the towers to the Trout Lake headquarters and the nearest town. Federal cooperation under the Weeks Law enabled the hiring of 11 seasonal fire patrolmen. In addition, the law authorized the federal government to purchase forestlands in the headwaters of navigable streams, established the National Forest Reservation Commission, gave consent for states to enter into compacts to conserve forests and water supplies, and authorized federal matching funds for approved state agencies to protect forested watersheds of navigable streams.[22]

REGIONAL COOPERATION BEGINS

Because similar conditions in the region called for uniform legislation, Griffith proposed a regional meeting. The first Lake States Forestry Conference convened at Saginaw, Michigan, in 1907, the second at Madison in 1908, and the third at St. Paul, Minnesota, in 1910. The conferences paid particular attention to the problem of forest fires. As a result of the meeting, private timber owners in Michigan and Wisconsin created the Northern Forest Protective Organization. The adoption of fire-protection systems did not solve the fire problem, but it did provide a beginning of

The State Forestry Headquarters at Trout Lake was an impressive combination of log construction and stone. It was ready for occupancy in October 1917, just as it became too cold to live in tents. The building provided living quarters, an office for the assistant state forester, and a men's dormitory. It was referred to as the "statehouse" and "the Headquarters for Forestry and Conservation" until the 1950s. The building was torn down in the mid-1960s.

31

STAR LAKE PLANTATION[3]

In 1913, E. M. Griffith chose a peninsula in Star Lake, in what is now the Northern Highland–American Legion State Forest, for the location of the first state plantation. The peninsula once served as a pasture for the horses of the Williams and Salsich Lumber Company, and the company had fenced it off. Because of its proximity to water and a ranger station, the site offered good protection from forest fires. Perhaps, too, Griffith wanted to show that what happened to Star Lake did not have to happen with good forest management. Star Lake had once been a thriving lumber town with a population of about 700. By 1908 it was a ghost town.

Griffith decided to plant mostly native red and white pine on the peninsula. Because many people questioned the effectiveness of reforestation, however, he included some Scotch pine, a fast-growing European species, to quickly convince the skeptics. Fred Wilson, state forest ranger, supervised the planting, which involved clearing an area about 18 inches square for each seedling with a grub hoe and hand planting the seedlings. Wilson developed a management plan for the plantation based on management and thinning procedures used in Europe. He decided that after thinning, the distance between the remaining trees should be 20 to 25 percent of the height of the dominant trees. The first thinning took place in 1943. In 1977, Wilson remeasured and marked the Star Lake Plantation for a thinning cut for the sixth time. His meticulous records on the plantation proved that tree planting paid off.

To demonstrate the value of reforestation, Griffith directed that a permanent and accurate record of the Star Lake Plantation be kept. To accomplish this, experimental plots were established, such as this one, which had been recently thinned to improve growth when this photo was taken.

These 8.4 cords of pulpwood came from just a single acre of the Star Lake Plantation during its fourth thinning in 1961— a graphic illustration of the value of reforestation.

cooperative efforts between the states and the federal government. The conferences resulted in no Wisconsin legislation except that Chapter 119, Laws of 1909, specifically authorized locomotive inspection, which some railroads had challenged, and empowered the state forester to order patrols to follow trains in periods of high hazard.[23]

1911 LEGISLATION

In his third biennial report, Griffith recommended a two-tenths mil tax (one mil is one-thousandth of a U.S. dollar) of assessed valuation for 20 years for forestry. Both the Committee on Waterpower, Forestry, and Drainage and the Conservation Commission endorsed his recommendation. Despite the favorable outlook when the legislature met in 1911, the program Griffith advocated was not adopted as introduced. Instead of appropriating $60,000 a year for 20 years, the legislature passed a bill providing $50,000 a year for a period of five years for purchase of land for the timber reserve.[24] More important, the action of the legislature signaled "the beginning of a long, sustained, vigorous, and sometimes unfair— sometimes downright dishonest—attack upon the forestry plans and any state policy which sought to limit the extent or nature of the use to be made of

the lands of northern Wisconsin."[25]

The most noteworthy development in the 1911 legislature was the approval of the State Conservation Commission, which functioned independently from the other agencies charged with conservation regulation. The commission consisted of seven members appointed to six-year terms by the governor. Its duty was to study the state's natural resources and submit a biennial report to the governor that included recommendations for conservation and a draft of any proposed legislation.[26]

STATE TAKES INITIATIVE IN FIRE PROTECTION AND CONSERVATION EDUCATION

In March 1911, the state held the first civil service examination for forest rangers. Of the 12 rangers appointed, F. G. Wilson was the only trained forester. During the field seasons of 1911 and 1912, 159.5 miles of road, 118 miles of fire lanes, and 56 miles of telephone line were completed. State Forester Griffith believed that this represented a greater amount of permanent protective work than had been established by any other state in an equal amount of time.[27]

In 1912, the state's first serious and consistent

attempt was initiated to educate schoolchildren and the general public about conservation. That year, Warden E. A. Cleasby spent his time speaking at schools and teachers' and farmers' institutes, and other wardens spent part of the winter months in the same work. These efforts increased in later years due to the public's enthusiastic response.[28]

In 1913, the legislature established the boundaries of the state forest reserve area to include some 1.25 million acres of intermingled state and private land in Vilas, Oneida, Forest, Price, and Iron Counties and laid out 12 protective districts. Under a new cooperative agreement with the federal government, Wisconsin received $5,000 of Weeks Law funds for fire protection with the understanding that the state would spend $15,000 of its own funds for this purpose. These funds made possible the hiring of 10 rangers and 9 seasonal patrolmen. They spent most of their time, however, on improvement work, and by 1915 they had completed 37 buildings, including a permanent headquarters building at Trout Lake, 250 miles of road, 140 miles of fire lanes, and 86 miles of telephone line.[29]

In 1915, Wisconsin became the first state to use an airplane for spotting fires. The first flight took place on August 2, 1915, from the Trout Lake headquarters in a Curtis Flying Boat with Jack Vilas

33

The Curtis Flying Boat allowed E. M. Griffith to become the first professional forester to detect fires from an airplane. Pictured here after the first flight on August 2, 1915, are (left to right) Neal Harrington, Lewis McLean, Ed Kiefer, Jack McDonald, Ellis Weaver, Pete Christensen, and pilot Jack Vilas. The photo was taken at the Trout Lake headquarters.

as pilot and forest ranger Ellis Weaver as observer. Vilas made almost daily flights during August and September and proved the feasibility of detecting fires from planes. Lack of communication with the ground and difficulty in flying in windy weather, however, limited the effectiveness of the plane for this purpose, and Griffith discontinued its use. It served, however, to give the state's fire-control effort considerable publicity.[30]

FOREST RESERVE GROWS

From the beginning, Griffith pursued a policy of developing a large state forest reserve, and by 1911 he had called for an area of two million acres. In addition to purchasing land with state funds, Griffith actively urged the federal government to turn over land to the state for forest reserves and encouraged private owners to give gifts to the state. By 1915, the amount of land acquired through federal and private grants and state purchase amounted to about 180,000 acres.[31]

FARMING THE CUTOVER

A number of individuals and groups opposed Griffith's forestry program. The most intense and effective opposition came from those individuals and groups whose economic interests conflicted with forestry. Railroad companies, real-estate agents, county politicians, land companies, and taxpayers of northern Wisconsin generally agreed that most of that part of the state should become farmland. For a time, some lumber companies tried to dispose of their cutover lands to settlers; many companies maintained their own land departments for this purpose. The state supported a strong and active immigration service for many years. Much of the land, however, remained unsold and eventually became tax delinquent. Attracted by the low land prices, speculators bought up large tracts, advertised them widely, and initiated a land boom.[32]

Despite the reports of Lapham and Roth, many scientists at the beginning of the twentieth century stressed the positive aspects of the Cutover for agricultural settlement. William A. Henry of the UW College of Agriculture, for example, supervised the establishment of three temporary substations of the college's experimental station in the Cutover in 1905. Two years later, E. J. Delwiche, a recent graduate of the college, began a series of winter meetings with farmers in Bayfield and Ashland Counties, which developed a statewide series of farmers' institutes. Between 1910 and 1913, about 20 percent of these institutes were held in communities in the Cutover. Harry L. Russell,

who had succeeded Henry as dean of the UW College of Agriculture in 1907, likewise encouraged the agricultural development of the Cutover. He established two permanent experimental substations at Ashland Junction in Bayfield County and at Spooner in Washburn County and reported that "the experimental fields showing the adaptability of this soil to wheat, pea, and clover culture are in full view of every passing train." Russell also used a 1909 state law authorizing the appointment of "itinerant" instructors and "traveling schools" to bring agricultural expertise to the Cutover. By 1915, 8 of the 13 such positions were in the Cutover counties, and 3 others were in adjacent counties.[33]

Russell assigned the state's first county agricultural agent to Oneida County in 1912. This agent, Ernest Luther, wrote confidently, "I think that it is up to me now to show the world how to farm jack pine land." Russell placed most of the first agricultural agents in northern Wisconsin counties and encouraged his faculty in Madison to work on the development of forage crops adapted to the short growing season in the Cutover.[34]

In 1913, the Wisconsin Advancement Association published a map prepared by the college's soil experts that showed how much land

Harry L. Russell studied in the laboratories of Koch and Pasteur and received his PhD at Johns Hopkins University. In 1893, he began his long career at the UW College of Agriculture. He believed that northern Wisconsin would become one of the nation's leading agricultural sections, even surpassing southern Wisconsin as a dairy center. His faith was so strong that he invested $35,000 of his own money in the Wisconsin Colonization Company. No one devoted himself more wholeheartedly to the development of the Cutover than Russell.

35

could be made into farms. However, Russell's lack of confidence in the state forester was evident. Writing to W. H. Webb, president of the Wisconsin Advancement Association, Russell declared that the soil surveys of the areas in question showed relatively larger amounts of fair, good, or excellent agricultural lands than had been supposed earlier. In the first two decades of the century, the Wisconsin Geological and Natural History Survey published studies of the Cutover that ranged from cautiously optimistic to strongly bullish about the region's resources and agricultural possibilities.[35]

For example, in a 1914 report on the Bayfield area, A. R. Whitson, with the Wisconsin Geological and Natural History Survey and his colleagues, recommended reforestation of less than 4 percent of the region and described the success of fruit cultivation near Bayfield and dairying near Ashland. The state sponsored and subsidized fairs to promote the agricultural potential of northern Wisconsin and encourage the efforts of its farmers. The Northern Wisconsin State Fair, at Chippewa Falls, began in 1897 largely as a showplace for northern Wisconsin agricultural products; the state initially had provided a subsidy of $2,500. Through the 1920s, the Northern Wisconsin State Fair received the most state aid of any fair in Wisconsin.[36]

ASSAULTS ON FORESTRY

By 1911, many northern Wisconsin newspapers had begun an assault on Griffith's forestry program. Under the hostile headline "State of Wisconsin Gobbles up 25,700 Acres of Best Land for Settlers," the *Rhinelander News* reported that the G. F. Sanborn Company had sold to the state more than 25,000 acres of land located in Vilas and Oneida Counties at $3.50 an acre. Early in 1912, the paper began a full-scale and continuing attack upon Griffith and the forest reserve program, and a year later the *New North* (formerly the *Vindicator of Rhinelander*) followed suit. Newspapers of other northern counties soon joined in the attack, and the debate became general when the *Wisconsin Agriculturist* gave its support to the antiforestry campaign.[37]

Opposition to Wisconsin's expanding forestry program, together with questions as to the legality of the State Board of Forestry's land-acquisition policy, led to the secretary of state's refusal to authorize payment on certain contracts entered into for the purchase of land for the forest reserve. The matter ended up in the Wisconsin Supreme Court for review and decision. On February 12, 1915, the state supreme court (state ex. rel. Owen v. Donald, 160 Wis 21) declared that the forestry

amendment of 1910 had been improperly adopted and was void because of a minor procedural error, the land purchase contracts were in conflict with the constitutional limitation against incurring indebtedness, and the administration of trust fund grant lands by the State Board of Forestry was an illegal invasion by the legislature of the trusteeship of the Commissioner of Public Lands, a constitutional body. The decision wiped out the forestry fund, reduced the forest reserve to lands granted or given to the state specifically for that purpose, and left the State Board of Forestry with only its annual appropriation to operate on. However, the supreme court decision did not affect fire prevention and control, and these functions continued.[38]

Some northern Wisconsin papers greeted the decision with delight. The editor of the *New North* declared that sentiment in the state was turning away from the forestry program anyhow, but the supreme court decision "drives the nail to the head at once and forever. . . . There would be many fine farms in the north now, and settlers and land buyers need have no fear of high taxes or isolation."[39]

GRIFFITH'S TENURE ENDS

In 1915, the legislature combined the activities of the Conservation Commission, the

State Board of Forestry, the State Park Board, the Fish Commission, and the state game warden under a new State Conservation Commission comprising three paid members: a trained forester, a fish and game warden, and a businessman.[40]

Governor Emanuel Philipp offered Griffith an appointment as the forestry member. But the supreme court decision greatly disappointed Griffith. He took it as a repudiation of his efforts, left Wisconsin, and severed all connections with the forestry profession.[41]

"Too much politics, causing the progress of the work to be retarded, is the reason I gave notice of my resignation as state forester," said Griffith. "Our state is rich in forests," he went on. "It is one of the greatest in the country. But continual interference on the part of state officials and constant changes in administration hinder the work.

"Wisconsin now has 360,000 acres of fine forestlands. I trust that the state will not be so foolish to give away these reserves to land speculators as she has on two previous occasions."[42]

While it lasted, Griffith's forestry program had made remarkable progress, but his ideas on forestry and land use proved 20 years ahead of their time. His departure and the court decision initiated a new chapter in Wisconsin forestry.

CHAPTER THREE

THE POST-GRIFFITH ERA (1915–1933)
FORESTRY RECEIVES DUE ATTENTION AND FUNDING

"WE HAVE JUST ADOPTED *a land use ordinance; we have our county forest, the first state forest has developed, and the plantation at Star Lake has become an attraction; we have industry forests owned by paper companies; and our recreation resources draw thousands, not only in summer. We have done everything Mr. Griffith advocated; he should have had our support."*

—Ole Rismon to Vilas County Board, 1933

FRANK MOODY—
A CAREER CUT SHORT

In July 1915, after E. M. Griffith declined the position of forestry member of the State Conservation Commission, Governor Emanuel Philipp appointed Frank Moody to the post. Moody, a graduate of the School of Forestry at the University of Michigan, served as assistant state forester under Griffith from 1906 to 1912 and then took a position at Cornell University. Moody carried on the work of the forestry division as energetically as possible within the restrictions imposed by the Wisconsin Supreme Court's 1915 decision.[1]

From 1915 through 1919, the Conservation Commission concentrated its meager resources in the general locale of the "state forest" in Forest, Vilas, Oneida, Price, and Iron Counties. Moody directed the preparation of a fire-protection plan for this region, which divided it into 17 protection districts, each with a ranger or seasonal patrol officer in charge. During droughts, patrolmen manned four primary lookout towers and patrolled along railroads and in the vicinity of settlements

Numerous writers considered stumps the most onerous obstacle to farming in the Cutover. Blasting with dynamite afforded an efficient means of stump removal, but its expense precluded its use by most Cutover settlers. However, the end of World War I provided an abundance of surplus explosives. For a few years, cheap explosives and high farm prices provided the hope that the Cutover would at last be converted to farms.

In addition to state agencies and lumber companies, land companies tried to lure farmers to the Cutover with "cheap" land, "free" stump-pulling services, and "at cost" agricultural supplies. More than 185 land colonization companies had home offices in Wisconsin after the turn of the century. When the *Forest Republican* announced the formation of the Per-Ola Land Company at Crandon in 1916, it told readers that the company would "operate under a plan that represents a distinctly new departure in the methods of converting cut-over lands into productive farms."

and resorts. Four auxiliary towers served for emergency use. The U.S. Indian Service cooperated by maintaining a lookout on the adjoining Lac du Flambeau Indian Reservation, and the Chicago & North Western Railroad and the C. H. Ferry estate financed patrols under state supervision to protect their property.[2]

In addition, Moody appointed the foremen and camp superintendents of six large lumber companies operating in the area to fight fires on or adjoining their lands. Lookout towers, a telephone system, and network of roads and trails started in 1911 facilitated protection. In 1918, Moody appointed seven patrol officers and assigned five of them to areas outside the proposed state forest reserve. Three of them each patrolled three counties, while the other two covered Vilas and Oneida Counties. Most of the patrol officers traveled in automobiles.[3]

The new forestry division was far from the organization that Griffith had hoped to create. Yet considering the effects of the 1915 supreme court decision and the disruption brought on by the country's entry into World War I in 1917, the new forestry division showed remarkable success. Moody greatly improved fire protection, expanded the Trout Lake Nursery, and pushed the work of reforestation. What would have transpired if Moody

had continued his work remains speculation because he died in August 1918 at the age of 38. C. L. Harrington succeeded him as forestry member of the Conservation Commission.[4]

PRESSURES FOR FARMLAND

The period from 1915 through 1920 saw tremendous activity directed at the agricultural settlement of the Cutover. During this period, interest in a policy to reserve some land for forestry and to prevent settlement on land obviously unsuitable for farms all but disappeared. With the high food prices caused by World War I and the desire to provide land for veterans after the war, groups that since the 1890s had urged, advocated, encouraged, and assisted the agricultural settlement of the Cutover came to the forefront. The 1910 census classified 6.5 percent of the total area of 17 northern counties as farmland. During the next 10 years, farm acreage increased at the rate of 63,850 acres per year. At such a rate, it would have taken 180 years to convert all the forestland into farmland.[5]

In 1921, Harry Russell, dean of the UW College of Agriculture, spoke glowingly about the immense amount of land still available for farms in northern Wisconsin—an empire of more than

10 million stumpland acres, of which 8.5 million were available for farmland. There was room and opportunity to start 100,000 farms on this land of adequate rainfall and good soil. Russell objected to governmental support and loans to farmers in the dryland sections of the western United States. Settlers in these regions were, he believed, gambling with nature. No such gamble, he claimed, was involved in farming in northern Wisconsin, which, he said, was a region where clover thrived as a weed and pastures remained green throughout the grazing season. Despite such optimistic pictures by Russell and the energetic support of numerous agencies, individuals, and groups, land clearing and the development of farms did not proceed rapidly in this "embryo empire."[6]

ABANDONED FARMS

A sharp decline in agricultural prices ushered in the 1920s. From 1921 to 1925, farm acreage decreased 13,200 acres per year in the Cutover. Concrete evidence of the failure of agriculture in the Cutover lands during the decade became obvious with the abandonment of farms, increased tax delinquency, and the slight flow of new farmers into the region. In 1921, one million acres (out of a total area of a little more than 11 million acres)

The UW College of Agriculture operated land-clearing demonstration trains to illustrate the use of dynamite for stump removal. In May 1916, the first "Land Clearing Special" made its run in the Cutover. The train traveled for two weeks and made 18 demonstrations. More than 8,000 settlers, some of them walking 25 miles, attended the demonstrations.

Second-growth birch and other trees on land where pine forest had been cut over near, 1929. Note the numerous large pine stumps scattered throughout the second-growth forest.

of land in the 17 northern Wisconsin counties had been offered for sale as tax delinquent. By 1927, the amount of land offered for tax sale reached 2.5 million acres, or about one-fourth of the total land area in the 17 counties.[7]

Knowingly or not, those who promoted farming in the Cutover had perpetrated a cruel hoax; more than 10,000 families failed at it. After 40 years of ardent work by real-estate dealers, county officials, state officials, faculty of the UW College of Agriculture, and land companies, only 6 percent of the total acreage consisted of cultivated crops in 1927. In 1928, Benjamin H. Hibbard, University of Wisconsin professor of agricultural economics, headed a study of taxation in the 17 northern counties, and the resulting report supported allegations that efforts to farm much of the Cutover land had been ill advised. By this time, even Russell had conceded that the attempt to extend agriculture into the Cutover had failed.[8]

As a result, efforts to reforest northern Wisconsin gained renewed momentum. In 1923, the U.S. Forest Service established the Lake States Forest Experiment Station at St. Paul, Minnesota, as a regional research agency with a staff that included five foresters. Its purpose was to develop a sound forestry program for the management of the

56 million acres of forestland in Michigan, Wisconsin, and Minnesota. Initially, the station directed its activities to problems of the Cutover area—reforestation, fires, and economic factors. In particular, it tried to provide information on effective planting techniques and their probable success under different conditions.[9]

THE BEGINNING OF INDUSTRIAL FORESTRY

In the mid-1920s, several paper and lumber companies laid the foundation for the development of industrial forestry. In 1923, the Consolidated Water Power & Paper Company planted spruce and pine seedlings in a barren field near Biron in an attempt to reforest burned-over land. During the summer of 1924, the Holt Lumber Company commissioned consulting foresters Banzhaf and Watson Inc. of Milwaukee to examine part of their timberland and to prepare a management plan for selective logging. In addition, the company sought the advice and assistance of Raphael Zon, director of the Lake States Forest Experiment Station.[10]

Late in the fall of 1924, the Holt Lumber Company cut 80 acres under its new management plan. The cut removed about 14 trees, or about 4,000 board feet of sawlogs, per acre. This was

VELEBIT: AN ABANDONED CUTOVER SETTLEMENT[1]

Many people know of the numerous ghost towns left in the wake of the lumbering era, and attempts to farm the Cutover also produced their share of abandoned settlements. A good example is Velebit, a Croatian farming community once located about eight miles east of Eagle River. Most of the Croatians settled there as a result of the encouragement of Joseph Habrich, a Croatian immigrant and an agent for the Sanborn Land Company. Habrich came to Eagle River in 1915 and over the next several years (1915–1925) helped 100 Croatian families settle at Velebit. Some of the immigrants named their settlement after their home near the Velebit Mountains in Yugoslavia.

Apparently the Sanborn Land Company used some deceitful advertising to lure settlers to Velebit. Some of its advertisements included a photo of a farm with a well-constructed house, a barn, and a concrete silo. Some of the immigrants expected to find a cleared farm, a house, a barn, and a cow on the land that they had bought. Instead they found a heavily forested or stump-filled tract of 40 acres with no buildings at all.

The settlers at Velebit primarily cultivated potatoes, corn, cabbage, and hay and kept cows, pigs, and chickens. Many of the men worked seasonally in local logging camps or sawmills to supplement their farm income. In addition to the farmsteads, Velebit eventually grew to include a school and a Croatian Fraternal Union Hall. As in much of the Cutover area, however, a short growing season and poor soils made farming a tenuous undertaking. By the late 1920s, unable to make a satisfactory living, many settlers had abandoned Velebit. Today, little remains of the settlement except for some ruins and foundations along mostly unpaved U.S. Forest Service roads and trails.

NEKOOSA-EDWARDS INDUSTRIAL FORESTRY[2]

In 1925, a survey classified 1,500–2,000 acres of land near Port Edwards and Nekoosa as nonproductive and another 2,000–3,000 acres as underproductive. As a result, the Nekoosa-Edwards Paper Company hired F. G. Kilp, one of the first industrial foresters in Wisconsin, and began the first industrial forestry program in the Lake States with the establishment of its Nepco Lake Tree Nursery. Until its nursery came into production, the company obtained jack pine and red pine seedlings from the U.S. Forest Service. In the first two years, the company planted some 100,000 trees. In 1927, its nursery produced 240,000 seedlings for replanting, and that year the company erected a 70-foot fire tower and acquired a Dodge fire truck with Evinrude fire pumps, Smith Indian fire pumps, shovels, pails, and axes. By 1930, the company had increased its annual planting to five million trees.

By the early 1940s, the company had planted 46 million trees and reforested 36,535 acres. As part of its reforestation program, Nekoosa-Edwards, in cooperation with the Wisconsin Conservation Department, initiated a pioneer program of insect- and disease-control research and prevention. In the mid-1940s, the company established two additional nurseries. Eventually, the company's reforested lands grew to more than 260,000 acres.

In 1966, the company began the Nekoosa Tree Farm Family. Through this program, Nekoosa Papers Inc. offered free advice, assistance, and consultation to private woodland owners to maximize the yield on reforested lands. In return, the landowner agreed to give Nekoosa Papers Inc. the first option to purchase the pulpwood off that land at the market price at the time of harvest.

about 35 percent of the acreage's volume. The company also removed about 100 cords of pulp and chemical wood (wood used for the production of such chemicals as acetic acid, methyl alcohol, and acetone). By the end of the winter of 1928, the Holt Lumber Company had cut about 900 acres on a selective basis. The company planned to cut another third of merchantable timber in 15 years, the expected time to replace the first cutting. Removal of the mature trees, however, greatly accelerated growth, and the tract was ready for a second cutting well before expected. In reporting on this experiment with selective cutting, the *American Lumberman*, an important trade journal, lauded its desirability but noted its "impracticability" in Wisconsin because of the state's tax structure, which encouraged companies to cut and get out.[11]

In 1927, the Connor Lumber Company of Laona, one of the largest in Wisconsin, announced its plan to start an extensive reforestation program. Initially the company planned to replant 40–60 acres of Cutover land a year. Later it increased the acreage to 100 acres a year. It planned to use trees from the Trout Lake Nursery. The company started planting in 1928 with 50,000 white pine and red pine seedlings. It intended to increase its planting to 100,000 seedlings in 1929. The company replanted areas unsuitable for agriculture and located near fire-prevention facilities.[12]

SEVEN STATE FORESTS DESIGNATED

While the state acquired some land in the early 1900s, it did not officially establish a state forest with definite boundaries until 1925. That year it established the Northern Highland State Forest, which originated from the forest reserve that the state had set aside in 1904 in Forest, Oneida, and Vilas Counties. Between 1925 and 1938, the state designated six additional state forests: American Legion, Flambeau River, Brule River, Kettle Moraine, Council Grounds, and Point Beach.[13]

Although the state forests were established primarily for growing timber and demonstrating forestry methods, it was recognized that "the scenic values, scientific and educational values, outdoor recreational values, public hunting and fishing opportunities, and the stabilization of stream flow are important extra benefits." Eventually, under the principle of multiple use, these forests contained special-use areas such as recreation sites, wilderness areas, scientific areas, and game refuges where such

uses took precedence over timber production.[14]

WISCONSIN SCHOOL FORESTS FIRST IN NATION

Almost simultaneously, another effort in the reforestation movement began. On a trip to Australia in 1925, Harry Russell, dean of the UW College of Agriculture, observed schoolchildren planting trees and thought this would be an excellent educational activity in the Wisconsin Cutover. Through Russell's efforts, the legislature passed a law in 1927 permitting school districts and municipalities to own land for and to engage in forestry. The following year the Laona and Crandon School Districts established the first school forests in the state and in the nation. The establishment of a school forest required that the school acquire through donation or other means 40 acres or more of land located adjacent to or near the school and that the land remain in perpetuity the property of the school. Each year, schoolchildren, under the direction of the forestry extension specialist from the College of Agriculture, had to replant a portion of the area and, if necessary, carry out thinning, clear a fire lane, and practice other sound management techniques.[15]

Under the leadership of Wakelin "Ranger

Students plant a tree as part of a dedication at the Laona School Forest, 1928.

45

Above: Wakelin McNeel's primary interest was in trees and forestry, and for many years he directed 4-H forestry and conservation activities and encouraged the school forest movement. In one year, he supervised the distribution of over one million trees to 4-H club members and vocational agriculture students for planting in farm nurseries and windbreaks.

Right: Aldo Leopold (1887–1948) is recognized as one of the preeminent leaders in the history of conservation, public land management, and environmental ethics. Author of *A Sand County Almanac*, Leopold influenced the passage of legislation and statewide conservation policies, the attitudes of political leaders, and trained a legion of wildlife managers to make the connection between wildlife and sound forest management.

Mac" McNeel of the 4-H Club Department of the Agricultural Extension (part of the UW College of Agriculture), the school forest movement grew quickly. By 1932, the state had 40 school forests and 21 school plantations. Meanwhile, the UW College of Agriculture initiated another program aimed at educating the state's schoolchildren about the importance of planting and protecting forests. In 1926, it began the Junior Forest Rangers to instruct boys of the state in forestry projects. By 1927, the Junior Forest Rangers had 600 members in 20 counties. That year they planted 130,000 trees, and many of them started small nurseries to grow trees for future plantings.[16]

The forestry education movement gathered more momentum when in 1935 the state legislature mandated conservation education at state high schools, vocational schools, universities, and colleges.[17]

ALDO LEOPOLD'S LAND ETHIC

As the true nature of northern Wisconsin's physical environment became known, the belief that the region needed new developmental policies grew stronger. Both directly and indirectly, the ideas of Aldo Leopold contributed to this rethinking.

Leopold earned his master's of forestry degree from Yale in 1909. Later that year he joined the U.S. Forest Service, and in 1924, he accepted a position with the Forest Products Laboratory in Madison. He founded the applied science of wildlife management and was a professor at the University of Wisconsin from 1933 through 1938.[18]

Aldo Leopold formulated the concept of a "land ethic"—the appreciation of the environment as a system, including both animals and vegetation. Leopold worked to develop this consciousness not only through his teaching and writing, but also in practice. On an abandoned farm that he bought in 1935 in Sauk County, he showed what could be done to restore the land.[19]

As early as 1925, Leopold argued that most remaining wilderness areas in the United States, like those in the "poor areas" of the Great Lakes states, were "entirely devoid of either existing or potential agriculture." He called for the retention of certain wild areas to "introduce a healthy variety into the wilderness idea itself."[20]

STATE'S FOREST TAX LAW A MODEL FOR THE NATION

In 1925, a state legislative committee on administration and taxation began a two-year investigation that led to the amendment of the uniform tax clause of the state constitution and to passage of the Forest Crop Law in 1927. Under this law, the owner of 160 or more acres (later reduced to 40 acres) could declare his or her land suited for forestry. If the State Conservation Commission approved, the land was entered under the Forest Crop Law, constituting a 50-year renewable contract between the owner and the state.[21]

Under the terms, the owner paid no property taxes except for an annual charge of 10 cents an acre. In return, he or she paid a severance tax of 10 percent of the value of the timber when cut. To compensate the town for lost property taxes, the state paid the town 10 cents per acre per year for lands in the forest crop program. Thus everyone benefited. This law has been called by some "the most forward-looking piece of forestland tax legislation ever enacted by an American legislature."[22]

During the first year of the law's operation, large lumber companies as well as individuals entered a total of 160,000 acres in the program. Reasonable forest taxation and adequate forest-fire protection encouraged lumber companies to abandon their cut-and-get-out policies. The Goodman Lumber Company was the first privately

R. B. Goodman, a member of the Wisconsin Conservation Commission, took an active part in the writing and passage of the Forest Crop Law and Rural Zoning Law and assisted in the organization of the Wisconsin Forest Fire Prevention System. In 1948, the American Forestry Association made him an honorary life member. An articulate spokesman for the lumbering industry as well as a leader in local government, Goodman helped lead the efforts to reforest northern Wisconsin.

THE GOODMAN FOREST[3]

By 1927, the Goodman Lumber Company had cut about half its virgin timber. That year, consulting foresters David Mason and Donald Bruce made a preliminary survey of the company's timberland, its cruiser's estimates of merchantable timber, and its detailed cover maps. Then Bruce outlined a management plan for sustained yield. The Goodman Lumber Company still had enough standing timber (hardwoods and hemlock) to convert to a sustained-yield operation. In 1927, the company established a forest nursery on an old pasture that adjoined the company farm. It began with 41 seedbeds of white pine, 13 white spruce, 7 red pine, and 7 elm.

In 1934, James W. Girard, assistant director of Forest Survey, U.S. Forest Service, examined the Goodman forest and wrote the following to C. A. Goodman, president of the Goodman Lumber Company: "Your forest practice is absolutely the finest I have seen anywhere in the entire country. I do not know of any operation that looks as good as your area. I have had an opportunity to see most of the selective logging in this country. Your job, when compared with all other operations which I have seen, stands out as the model operation."

In 1951, members of the Wisconsin Conservation Commission toured the timberland of the Goodman Lumber Company. Allen Haukon, executive secretary of the Forestry Advisory Committee, wrote, "The Commission saw here a model of sustained yield practiced by a private company which has maintained a stable, prosperous community, an essential, diversified forest industry, and a healthy, vigorous and beautiful forest."

When the Goodman Lumber Company sold its operation to Calumet & Hecla Inc. in 1955, it owned 70,000 acres of timberland that it managed under selective cutting. The transaction included a stipulation that the new owners continue sustained-yield forestry for 20–30 years under the provisions of the Forest Crop Law. In 1983, Goodman Forest Industries Ltd. reacquired the operations and timberland.

The eighth cutting cycle on the original Goodman Lumber Company land took place in 1999. From 1927 through 1999, 417 million board feet of timber had been removed. Yet the tract still contained about the same volume of timber that it had in 1927.

owned forest industry to adopt sustained yield in Wisconsin. In 1927, R. B. Goodman, secretary of the Goodman Lumber Company, decided to turn to sustained yield (managing lands for permanent timber production) and selective cutting, or, as he referred to it, a logging budget cutting only a part of the estimated annual growth, cutting out crowded stands, cutting only mature trees, and leaving new growth.[23]

CHANGES IN CONSERVATION COMMISSION

In 1927 the state legislature replaced the full-time, paid conservation commissioner with a policy-forming, nonsalaried body of six members to establish the Conservation Department with a conservation director as chief executive officer of the commission to administer conservation activities. The governor, with consent of the state senate, appointed two members biennially for six-year terms to the commission. [24]

CREATION OF COUNTY FORESTS

In 1927, the Wisconsin legislature enacted the County Forest Reserve Law as one method of reforesting land suitable only for growing trees.

Counties owned extensive tracts of land that they had acquired for nonpayment of taxes. The County Forest Reserve Law authorized counties to engage in forestry and laid the foundation for a system of county-owned forests that has been unique in the United States. Langlade County established the state's first county forest in 1928. In 1929, the legislature allowed tax-delinquent land to be put into county forests and entered under the Forest Crop Law. In 1930, for example, Marinette County entered more than 14,000 acres that it had acquired by purchase, tax deed, and trade. These laws provided a means for making use of idle tax-delinquent lands.[25]

ZONING AS AN AID TO FORESTRY

The efforts toward a more rational development of the Cutover did not end with the Forest Crop and County Forest Reserve Laws. In January 1928, the Marinette County Board of Supervisors adopted a resolution establishing a farm- and forestland survey committee and directing the committee to cooperate with the UW College of Agriculture and with county and town officers in the development of an economic survey for Marinette County. The resulting survey tabulated agricultural development, local tax expenditures, assessed valuations, and roads and schools by township from 1914 to 1928. It contained maps of soils, settlement, crop acreage, forest areas, and idle land.[26]

In May 1929, the University of Wisconsin–Extension published the results in a circular entitled "Making the Most of Marinette County Land." Its success led other counties to request similar studies. Between April 1931 and April 1934, the UW–Extension published the results of such studies for Ashland, Taylor, Oneida, Forest, Washburn, and Langlade Counties. This series culminated in the 1934 publication of "Making the Best Use of Wisconsin Land Through Zoning."[27]

Meanwhile, in December 1928, representatives from the 17 northern counties met at Rhinelander to consider recommendations for legislation for a more rational development of the Cutover lands. Out of this conference came a proposal that each county should receive authority to establish land-use zones within county lines.[28]

Based on this proposal, in April 1929, assemblyman Joseph D. Grandine of Forest County submitted a bill to provide counties with the authority to "regulate, restrict, and determine the areas within which agriculture, forestry, and recreation may be conducted." After the Wisconsin legislature passed the bill, L. G. Sorden, Oneida County agent, noted the significance of this action. "This zoning ordinance," he wrote, "is the first ordinance of its kind to be enacted in the United States. . . . We believe this zoning ordinance will pave the way for sounder development in localities close to roads, close to schools, and close to markets. We also believe it will be a forerunner of a land utilization policy by other counties and perhaps other states." His words proved prophetic. Two northern counties completed their zoning ordinances in 1933, 16 in 1934, 5 in 1935, and 7 between 1936 and 1940. Within two decades, 38 states had adopted enabling acts, and by 1951 one-third of the counties in the United States had authority to zone.[29]

After the 1927 constitutional amendment, the Forest Crop Law, and the County Forest Reserve Law, the need for better fire protection became increasingly urgent so that these reforestation devices could have their desired effect. Accordingly, the legislature completely overhauled the Forest Protection District Law and gave the State Conservation Commission the overall direction of protection activities. It vested the commission "with power, authority, and jurisdiction

49

While much of the land that became part of the Chequamegon–Nicolet National Forest had been cutover and/or burned, some consisted of remnant forest. This uncut stand of hardwoods and hemlock was part of the Oneida purchase for the Nicolet National Forest.

in all matters relating to the prevention, detection, and suppressions of forest fires outside the limits of incorporated villages and cities in the state, and to do all things necessary in the exercise of such power, authority, and jurisdiction." In 1928, northern Wisconsin had 10 organized fire-prevention districts, each supervised by full-time, well-trained personnel. Seventy-two steel lookout towers and a considerable amount of new trucks, pumps, and other equipment greatly improved the state's fire-control program.[30]

NATIONAL FORESTLAND ESTABLISHED IN STATE

Meanwhile, federal efforts at reforestation in Wisconsin started. The federal government began to buy cutover land in the eastern part of the United States in 1911 under the Weeks Law to protect the flow of navigable streams. In 1924, the enactment of the Clarke-McNary Law provided more federal aid for forest-firefighting, the promotion of farm forestry, and enlargement of federal forests. While the Wisconsin legislature made some efforts to induce the establishment of federal forests within the state, they did not lead to immediate federal action. In 1925, the Wisconsin legislature authorized the federal government to acquire up to 100,000 acres

in the state for a national forest, with the stipulation that the governor, the commissioners of public lands, and the Conservation Commission approve the selected area. Two years later, the legislature increased the allowable federal purchase to 500,000 acres, with the stipulation that the appropriate county board approve the purchase as well.[31]

By 1933, the federal government had authority to acquire up to two million acres in the state. Federal buying agencies moved slowly even after the National Forest Reservation Commission established buying areas. In December 1928, the commission approved the Oneida purchase unit of 151,680 acres in Oneida, Forest, and Vilas Counties.[32]

The first purchases from the Thunder Lake Lumber Company occurred in 1930. J. D. Mylea, president of the company, probably did more than any other individual to get a national forest established in Wisconsin. The U.S. Forest Service set up an office in Park Falls in 1929. S. D. Anderson headed the office and oversaw the management of the unit and the acquisition of additional lands. By 1935, the federal government had purchased almost 700,000 acres in the state for designation as national forestland.[33]

It was not only the state and federal

governments that contributed to the growth of forestry in this period. The Wisconsin Commercial Forestry Conference met in Milwaukee in March 1928. D. C. Everest, general manager of the Marathon Paper Mills Company, succinctly stated the purpose of the conference: "To forcefully bring to the attention of the timber owner, the timber user, and the general public the urgent necessity of replenishing the forests and making the growing of a timber crop as practical and as profitable as any agricultural crop."[34]

Leading representatives of the lumber industry, foresters, economists, and other experts attended the conference and examined the whole subject of forestry in the state in a series of papers published later in 1928 as "Forestry in Wisconsin: A New Outlook." "It was one of the influences which helped launch Wisconsin upon a permanent, sound, and carefully planned program of forest development," according to M. W. Swenson, president of the Wisconsin Chamber of Commerce, who attended the second conference in 1954.[35]

FORESTATION TAX A MAJOR STEP FORWARD

Wisconsin continued along a road of sound planning when in 1930 it exercised for the first time the authority of the 1924 constitutional amendment to levy a tax of one-twentieth of a mil on all taxable property to raise $298,797 for the acquisition, development, and protection of forest areas in the state. This was one of the most important events in Wisconsin forestry because implementation of the mil tax (also known as the forestation tax) provided a continual source of funding for forestry. Previously, forestry costs were paid from the general appropriation to the Conservation Commission.[36]

FIRE PROTECTION RECEIVES DUE FUNDING

Shortly after implementation of the mil tax, chief fire warden Fred Wilson was employed to organize and supervise forest-fire prevention and suppression activities. In 1931, the state legislature granted the Conservation Commission $600,000, most of it for forest protection. For the first time, ample funds were available to build and equip an effective fire-protection system. Moreover, public attitudes toward forest fires had changed after the general failure of agriculture in the Cutover. Coupled with various programs of the New Deal, this led to another chapter in the history of Wisconsin forestry.[37]

The early fire lookout towers essentially consisted of modified windmill towers with a platform and railing. Later a canvas roof was added. When a ranger spotted a fire, he had to climb down the tower to telephone his report to headquarters.

51

CHAPTER FOUR

THE REBIRTH OF THE FOREST (1933–1945)
WORKING TOWARD SUSTAINABILITY

"TO OLDTIMERS *whose memories reach back 30 years or more, the term 'cutover' has a great deal of meaning. It was applied to the fire-scarred stump and brush land that largely comprised northern and central Wisconsin. Now the word is little used. With effective forest protection, much tree-planting and a start on management, Wisconsin once again has forests. The cutover, in the old sense, belongs to history."* —*Wisconsin Conservation Bulletin*, February 1960

By the early 1930s, significant changes were under way, eventually culminating in the rebirth of Wisconsin's forestland. One such change was the creation and launching of the federal Civilian Conservation Corps (CCC) early in 1933.

With Congress's passage of the Emergency Conservation Work Act in 1933, President Franklin D. Roosevelt launched the Civilian Conservation Corps. This federal works program provided many of the country's unemployed youth with constructive, long-term conservation work, of which tree planting and forest-fire protection

were high priorities. The federal government established camps of approximately 200 men each within the state fire-protection districts and 24 additional camps on the national forests and Indian reservations. The establishment of the CCC meant that an adequate workforce for fire control was finally available. It also meant that more equipment to supplement the hand tools was available—tractors and plows to build fire lines and pumpers to move water from streams and lakes onto fires.[1]

Thanks to the CCC, the means for fire

CCC workers cut brush along the outside edge of a fire located northwest of Mercer in 1936.

CIVILIAN CONSERVATION CORPS CAMPS[1]

The federal government established CCC camps of approximately 200 men each within the state fire protection districts and 24 others on the national forests and Indian reservations. The 643rd Company Camp was located at Virgin Lake near Three Lakes.

In 1932, U.S. citizens elected Franklin D. Roosevelt president in a landslide vote. The nation was desperate for relief from the Great Depression, and Roosevelt quickly created dozens of programs to create jobs and stimulate the economy. One of these, authorized on May 5, 1933, was Civilian Conservation Corps (CCC). To be eligible for the CCC, men had to be 18–25 years old and single, with some member of their family receiving public relief. They received $30 per month, $24 of which they were to send to their families. Army-style camps were built in state and national parks and forests and other areas across the nation, where the men worked in reforestation, water conservancy, erosion control, park development, forest-fire protection, and other environmental endeavors.

CCC camps typically had eight local experienced men (LEM) who were local loggers or state and private foresters who had lost their jobs as a result of the Great Depression. Because most CCC enrollees had no experience in the woods, the LEMs proved to be of immense importance.

Wisconsin had an average of 54 camps a year, distributed as follows:

national forests, 26; state forests, 19; Soil Conservation Service, 17; and state parks, 14. Between 1933 and 1942, the CCC employed 92,094 men at Wisconsin camps, almost 64,000 of them from Wisconsin.

The CCC camps began to fold after war broke out with Japan. With the end of the CCC, many of the camp buildings were sold to contractors who tore them down for the material. Others were turned over to nearby communities. Some were simply abandoned.

The CCC left an enduring legacy in the many improvements it made, which the public still benefits from today in Wisconsin. The CCC constructed 483 bridges, erected 4,040 miles of telephone lines, built 4,396 miles of roads and fire lanes, planted 265,631,000 trees, expended 269,447 man-days fighting forest fires, and stocked 517,792,648 fish. The CCC put up fire lookout towers and improved forest stands. Other work included building ranger stations, manning fire towers, disease and insect control, landscaping, recreational area development, and improvement of wildlife habitat.

control appeared almost overnight, and impressive complexes of firebreaks became a fundamental component of fire-fighting strategy. But equally significant was the experience of fighting fires with large, organized crews.[2]

The public remembers the CCC most for its reforestation work. Indeed, a popular nickname for the CCC was "Roosevelt's Tree Army." In the fall of 1934, the CCC planted more than 6.5 million trees on 6,500 acres of the Nicolet National Forest. Two years later, it planted 16 million trees on 16,000 acres.

The economic benefit of the CCC's work continues to increase even today. The 39,000 acres of surviving CCC red pine plantings in the Chequamegon-Nicolet National Forest have an estimated value of $156 million, not counting the millions of dollars of pulpwood and sawtimber products already removed in thinnings that began in the 1960s. Today, improved forests and plantations established by the CCC in Wisconsin's state forests and parks, national forests, and Indian reservations are testimony to the effectiveness of this conservation program.[3]

COOPERATING INTERESTS

The same year as the start of the Civilian Conservation Corps, the University of Wisconsin College of Agriculture and the Wisconsin Conservation Department began working cooperatively on studies of forest nursery improvement, tree diseases, forest insects, and forest genetics. The Conservation Department contributed most of the financing and assisted in field operations, while the university provided personnel and facilities. On some projects, the federal government and/or private industries provided aid.[4]

SHELTERBELTS BECOME WIDESPREAD

In 1934, dust and sand storms devastated parts of central Wisconsin. The Wisconsin Conservation Department quickly initiated a 10-year-long shelterbelt project, in which a single strip of trees protects land from strong winds. An existing shelterbelt provided conclusive evidence of the effectiveness of such plantings in reducing wind erosion. In the spring of 1926, private landowners George and Ed O'Connor, at the suggestion of Fred Wilson, University of Wisconsin–Extension forester, planted a shelterbelt near Hancock to reduce wind erosion. It consisted of 3,000 white pines, three rows wide

During the 1930s, a severe drought exacerbated the problem of wind erosion in parts of Wisconsin, particularly in the sandy plains of central Wisconsin. As a result, the Wisconsin Conservation Department embarked on a shelterbelt program. This shelterbelt between Cambridge and Jefferson is typical of those planted during the 1930s.

and a mile long, that the O'Connors had obtained from the Trout Lake Nursery. When the state started its own shelterbelt program, it used the O'Connor shelterbelt as a model, and that shelterbelt set the pattern for many more. The Wisconsin Conservation Department furnished stock and, with the assistance of the University of Wisconsin–Extension, helped establish almost 6,000 miles of shelterbelts by 1944.[5]

FIRE PROGRAM CONTINUES TO EVOLVE

The fire season of 1934 marked the end of the prolonged drought and a turning point in Wisconsin's forest-fire history. Beginning in 1935, the Conservation Department emphasized building an effective organization with efficient personnel to prevent fires and provide adequate equipment to detect and quickly suppress fires. The state inaugurated a system of special emergency fire wardens with up to five wardens in each county. These officers patrolled all back roads, trout streams, lakes, camping grounds, and other places where people might create a fire hazard. They tagged cars with a special warning that explained the fire hazard and fire laws. As state officers, these wardens could enforce fire laws

Fire engines evolved to allow the transport of water to a forest fire for quicker and more effective response.

The innovation of the tractor and fire plow combination in the 1930s began the era of mechanized forest-fire suppression.

regardless of county lines. Under another cooperative plan with the state, the counties employed special deputy sheriffs for the same purpose. By 1936, fire towers had been erected 10–15 miles apart throughout the forest-protection districts. In periods of high hazard and low visibility, secondary lookout towers augmented the primary system.[6]

The decade from 1930 to 1940 was largely one of development and intensifying of existing fire-protection efforts rather than of expansion. With minor modifications and adjustments, the area under protection remained the same, but the Conservation Department strengthened the district organizations, acquired needed equipment, and inaugurated a training program for permanent and seasonal employees. It also gave more attention to fire prevention and law enforcement. In 1936, the Conservation Commission authorized the use of chartered airplanes for fire detection to supplement the lookout towers and for reconnaissance of ongoing fires. In 1938, an airplane hangar, a landing field, and a dock for seaplanes were constructed at Tomahawk. An airplane, a Stinson "station wagon," was purchased in 1947. It proved to be of inestimable value for both sizing up the fire

After 1934, the impact of organized fire control on the public's attitude toward forest fires resulted in greater care with fire in the woods and a drop in the annual number of fires. However, it did not entirely eliminate fires like this one in Marinette County.

AN EXPERIMENT IN FOREST-FARM RESETTLEMENT[2]

The Ernie Popp family moves into the Drummond Forest resettlement community.

As part of Franklin Roosevelt's New Deal, the federal government initiated a number of projects to relocate isolated Cutover settlers to better land within the Cutover where they could combine subsistence farming with work in the expanding network of county, state, and federal forests. The Drummond Forest Community, consisting of 32 home units within the Chequamegon National Forest, was one such project. The Resettlement Administration (later the Farm Security Administration) and the U.S. Forest Service started the project in 1935. Project officials chose a location about seven miles southwest of the town of Drummond in Bayfield County for relocation of nearby, isolated rural families. The location had soil suitable for agriculture as well as accessibility to forest work, good roads, a modern school, and a market for farm produce.

The project had three main objectives. Foremost was the relocation and rehabilitation of families living in isolated areas with no adequate sources of income. Second was to develop a skilled, reliable, and easily accessible source of labor for rehabilitation of lands recently acquired for the Chequamegon National Forest. Third, the project attempted to develop a model of combined forest and agricultural work that might work in much of the Cutover lands.

Each unit of the project consisted of 20 acres of land with 5 acres cleared for crops and 5 acres brushed for pasture. The houses (23 with four rooms and 9 with three rooms) consisted of neat frame buildings with modern plumbing. Each unit had a combination barn-garage. From August 1930 to the end of 1940, the community had near-full occupancy. The opening up of defense jobs and profitable work outside the community, however, caused occupancy to drop to about 20 percent between 1943 and 1944. As a result, the government decided to terminate the experiment and sell the homesteads to the residents. The Drummond project was an imaginative and relatively well-managed effort, but unexpected improvement in the economy brought on by World War II undermined it.

situation and directing the work of ground crews working on large fires.[7]

RAPID GROWTH OF INDUSTRIAL FORESTRY

With the decrease in fires and passage of the Forest Crop Law, industrial forestry rapidly expanded. In 1936, for example, the Consolidated Water Power & Paper Company conducted the largest logging operations in Langlade County. Under the direction of E. B. Hurst, its chief forester, the company selectively cut a tract of 18 "forties" (720 acres). The company owned about 30,000 acres of Cutover land in Forest, Langlade, and Oconto Counties and by 1941 had planted five million seedlings on the land. Consolidated accomplished this impressive total despite the fact that it sold most of its nursery production for 1934 and 1935 to the federal government for use by the CCC.[8]

In 1944, various wood-using companies organized the Forest Industries Information Committee to foster industrial forestry in the state. The committee's major purpose was to encourage the growing of trees commercially under proper management methods. The group was instrumental in establishing Certified Industrial Forests, tracts of land of 1,000 acres or more maintained for permanent tree growth under standards approved by the Conservation Commission.[9]

TAKING BACK THE LAND

Federal, state, and county governments in Wisconsin in the 1930s implemented relocation programs to move isolated settlers from marginal farms and to reduce the cost of services and relief for the counties. When counties adopted zoning ordinances, residents inside the areas zoned against farming were recorded as "nonconforming" users. As long as they continued to own and occupy the property, they could not be legally removed. This right belonged only to the settler who held and occupied the property at the time of zoning, but it ended when the settler left or sold out. Farmers were living in isolated areas with no adequate source of income. Such a life was particularly hard on children. Both economic and humanitarian reasons dictated that steps be taken to encourage nonconforming users to move out of the forests. Marinette County was the first county to take such steps. In January 1934, the Marinette County Board passed a resolution that instructed the county agent to assist in the relocation of isolated settlers by either land exchange or purchase.

The county made its first purchase in January 1936 when it bought five homesteads at Taylor Rapids. Between 1936 and 1944, the county purchased 16 farms, totaling 1,120 acres, for less than $14,000.[10]

The establishment by the federal government of the resettlement program provided funds to purchase marginal lands. Between 1934 and 1943, the Northern Wisconsin Isolated Settler Relocation Project spent $500,000 in federal money to purchase more than 400 farms in seven Cutover counties. Some 30–40 percent of the relocated settlers remained in farming. L. G. Sorden, project director, claimed that with the supervision given in their farming operations, most farmers succeeded on their new farms. The rest found nonfarm work in the Cutover area, took factory work in the cities, or retired.[11]

Some of the nonfarm work that settlers found included lumber-industry jobs created by the establishment of national forests. By the 1930s, the newly established national forests in Wisconsin were producing lumber and pulpwood. During 1939, timber sales from the Nicolet National Forest totaled 10,580,000 board feet. All of the timber was cut under approved forestry methods and provided enough labor to support 1,295 people, according to Forest Supervisor Galen W. Pike.

Five years later, the cut grew to over 14 million board feet to assist the war effort.[12]

GROWING FOR THE FUTURE

In 1944, as an outgrowth of wartime campaigns to step up pulpwood production, nine paper companies founded Trees For Tomorrow Inc. to literally grow more trees for tomorrow. The companies realized the need to assist private woodland owners to provide wood for the forest industry. At that time, Wisconsin's paper industry imported 80 percent of its needed pulpwood. Initially, the organization, with Melvin "Mully" Taylor as director, focused on expanded reforestation, technical assistance to forest landowners, and conservation education.[13]

Early projects included a reforestation institute in Rhinelander, the initiation of a free tree distribution plan, and the establishment of forestry scholarships. Recognizing the need for forests that could function as laboratories as well as commercial tracts of timber, the organization helped establish the Merrill Memorial Forest, the Oneida County Memorial Forest, and more than 30 school forests. Financing for the organization's activities came primarily from the supporting industrial firms, supplemented by donations and workshop fees.[14]

Director Melvin Taylor had a background in newspapers, and he persuaded the Wisconsin Press Association (now the Wisconsin Newspaper Association) to hold an annual meeting with Trees For Tomorrow to discuss the implications of resource management to the newspaper industry. The press association invested several thousand dollars to plant 50,000 trees in a demonstration forest located near Eagle River to illustrate the effects of forest management.[15]

FIRE-FIGHTING CHALLENGES

With the start of World War II, federal projects that were not associated with the war effort received little support from the government or the public. Like many agencies, the CCC came under review of Congress in 1941 and was disbanded in 1942. At the same time, wartime demand for forest products and fewer people available to fight fires made forest fires an even bigger problem. Greater emphasis was placed on trained standby crews to fight fires rather than on town fire wardens. These standby crews involved volunteer firefighters who were organized as an auxiliary forest-firefighting force.[16]

Between 1937 and 1942, some 30 million acres of forest- and rangeland burned annually in the United States. Because 90 percent of the fires were caused by humans, they might have been preventable. As a result, state and federal forestry agencies organized the Cooperative Forest Fire Prevention Campaign in 1942 to educate the American public. It sought assistance of the Wartime Advertising Council (later the Advertising Council Inc.), which came up with the Smokey Bear ad campaign. This effort proved so popular that Smokey continued as an important symbol of fire prevention after the war and remains so today.[17]

GOALS ACHIEVED

By 1945, zoning, the removal of isolated settlers, the establishment of county and other public forests, the expansion of industrial forestry, large technical advances in wood use, the improvement of fire-fighting techniques, readjustment of the tax burden, the work of the CCC, and the large expansion of the recreation business had combined to cause the rebirth of the forest. This set the stage for the next chapter in Wisconsin's forest history.

SMOKEY BEAR[3]

The Advertising Council Inc. and the U.S. Forest Service realized early on that the long-term success of their campaign to prevent forest fires depended on educating the nation's youth. As a result, they directed much of their efforts at schoolchildren. Here, Smokey Bear visits a Milwaukee school in 1954.

In 1944, Albert Staehle portrayed a bear in a ranger's hat and firefighter's dungarees as part of the Wartime Advertising Council's campaign to prevent forest fires. His rendition successfully blended the emotional appeal of an animal and the ruggedness of a firefighter. The bear was named Smokey. The council introduced his best-known slogan, "Only You Can Prevent Forest Fires," in about 1947. In 1950, a bear cub rescued from a forest fire in Lincoln National Forest in New Mexico and taken to the National Zoological Park in Washington, D.C., became the living symbol of forest-fire prevention.

Smokey Bear, as everyone knows, became a national icon. But not everyone knows about Wisconsin's place in the Smokey saga. During the 1950s, forest rangers in Wisconsin received many requests from local communities to enter floats in their parades. In 1950, W. S. Carow, district forest ranger at Mercer, received a request to enter a float in the firefighter's convention parade at Hurley, Wisconsin, and Ironwood, Michigan. Frank Brunner, conservation aid, constructed a stuffed, wooden-headed Smokey for the parade. The float depicted Smokey praying beneath a sign that read, "And please make people careful, Amen," surrounded by various forest animals.

The success of the float in the Hurley-Ironwood parade led Bernard Klugow to suggest making a Smokey suit that a man could wear. Neal Long, Frank Brunner, and Ada Hart used bear hides to fabricate a suit that made its first appearance in the Logging Congress parade at Wausau in September 1950. Three years later, Thomas Schucks, Conservation Department employee, spearheaded the creation of a bigger and better Smokey Bear costume. By the late 1950s, Wisconsin forest rangers had four Smokey Bear costumes that they used to help educate the public about fire prevention. The success of these efforts is demonstrated by a comment heard again and again by the rangers who accompanied Smokey. "Were you the forest ranger who came to our school? My children saw you and Smokey Bear, and that's all they talk about. Can't even burn garbage in my backyard without having one of them asking if I'm sure it's safe."

61

CHAPTER FIVE

POST–WORLD WAR II DEVELOPMENT (1945–1960)
WISCONSIN EXPANDS ITS ROLE IN FOREST MANAGEMENT

"WE RECOGNIZE *the need of proper forestry practice; that this state was built out of our forests, and is and will in the future be dependent on our forest, not only for the state's economy, but also for its recreation and its well being."*

—Charles D. Smith, Wisconsin Conservation Commissioner, 1960

After World War II, an organized effort developed to extend forestry throughout the state. In 1946, the Wisconsin Conservation Department hired two foresters to give technical assistance to private woodland owners, and in 1947 it established seven timber-harvest forests, later called demonstration forests.[1]

The seven forests ranged in size from 32 to 94 acres. From 1945 to 1950, activity on them was intense, with harvests conducted annually or nearly so on most of the seven tracts. These were typically followed by well-attended field days and often excellent press coverage. The harvests had the objective of focusing farmer attention on frequent cropping of the current timber growth from well-managed woodlands and demonstrating how additional income could be generated in the off-season.[2]

THE FORESTRY ADVISORY COUNCIL

In 1947, the State Conservation Commission established a Forest Advisory Council to advise the commission and the Wisconsin Conservation Department about forestry problems in the state. During its period of operation (1947 through the

The Northern Highland State Forest, established in 1925, and the American Legion State Forest (left), established in 1929, constitute a gross land area of approximately 714 square miles and are located in the central lakes region of Vilas, Iron, and Oneida Counties.

THE WAUSAUKEE TIMBER-HARVEST FOREST[1]

Forestry demonstrations occupied a place of primary importance at Marinette County's three-day Farm Progress Days program in the summer of 1959. Some 2,500 people toured the Wausaukee timber-harvest forest. There, the Wisconsin Conservation Department, in cooperation with other state agencies, the wood-using industry, and the U.S. Forest Service, provided a series of "listening points" along a half-mile-long trail.

At each stop, visitors learned about up-to-date forestry methods and such related activities as proper slash disposal, control of forest insects and diseases, treating fence posts, marking trees for harvest, portable sawmill operations, "box-piling" lumber, and hand-versus machine-planting of nursery-grown pine.

Few of those touring this 32-acre pine woods knew that it had been cut seven times in 11 years to yield products with a gross value of $3,500. Nor did they know that the sawtimber volume had increased by 46 percent. Fire protection and sound forestry practices made this growth possible.

The cooperation of three public agencies made this project a success. The University of Wisconsin Agricultural Extension was responsible for educational uses of the forest, including demonstrations at timber harvest field days. The Lake States Forest Experiment Station, U.S. Forest Service, maintained continuous records of tree growth and shared in the technical direction of the work. The Wisconsin Conservation Department, which held title to the lands, determined the disposition of the trees cut in successive timber harvests. The story of the Wausaukee timber harvest-forest represents, in a somewhat broader sense, nine other similar publicly owned and managed timber-harvest forests in Wisconsin. All of them demonstrate graphically the value of sustainable forestry.

late 1980s), the council made 57 recommendations, and the commission or the Natural Resources Board adopted all of them.[3]

TAX BREAKS AND ASSISTANCE FOR WOODLAND OWNERS

The passage by Congress of the Cooperative Forest Management Act of 1950 greatly stimulated farm forestry. It provided a strong and effective cooperative program to bring technical services to private woodland owners and operators, both in forest management and in the harvesting and marketing of timber. More important, it provided states with funds to hire personnel to set up management programs for landowners and timber producers.[4]

In 1952, farm woodlands accounted for 41 percent of the private woodlands in Wisconsin. That same year, in response to heavy demand for services, the farm-forestry project was expanded to 11 projects.[5]

The following year, Wisconsin's Woodland Tax Law permitted the owner of any tract of forestland of fewer than 40 acres and "not more suitable to any other purpose" to apply for annual taxes, payable to the town assessor, limited to

20 cents per acre for 10 years. Yield-tax payments at the time of harvest were not required. In exchange, the owner or operator agreed to promote the growing of trees and to refrain from grazing and burning on the entered lands, and the conservation director agreed to assist with planting and forest-management plans on request. The director submitted an annual report about forest practices on each tract. If the landowner did not practice forestry or if other uses prevailed, the director had authority to cancel the entry. In addition, the owner, town, or county board had the right to petition for a public hearing to have an entry canceled. On June 30, 1957, Wisconsin had 1,786 entries under the Woodland Tax Law.[6]

In 1954, the Conservation Commission adopted a policy to promote an even more aggressive program of small-woodland management. It hoped to ensure the cooperation of all interested or responsible public agencies in small-woodland management; recognize the importance of farmland timber production in conjunction with other multiple woodland values including wildlife habitat; and urge the removal of cows and other farm animals from grazing the woodlands.

In 1955, the Conservation Department assigned 11 foresters to farm forestry districts in the southern half of the state. The addition of the Special Classification provision of the Forest Crop Law in 1950 and the passage of the Woodland Tax Law in 1953 gave additional impetus to landowner assistance. The Forest Crop Law Special Classification provision allowed entry of holdings over 40 acres "outside of the intensive fire protection districts" and did not require payment of a severance tax.[7]

Of the 37 district foresters and assistants of the forest-management division in the field in 1955, 20 worked in 44 primarily agricultural counties. From 1953 to 1957, the farm forestry staff gave technical assistance to 13,000 owners with 351,000 acres of woodland. In addition, Conservation Department foresters, who primarily worked on county forest management, provided assistance to an average of 300 owners per year.[8]

Conservation Department foresters presented 824 forestry lectures, tours, and demonstrations and participated in the resource-management workshops at Trees For Tomorrow to interest forest landowners in the management program. By the late 1950s, the forest-management division of the Wisconsin Conservation Department employed 53 foresters, 35 of which worked exclusively on private land. They provided such assistance as

The American Tree Farm System of private timberland management, launched in 1941, encouraged sound forest management, particularly by owners of small woodlots. By 1961, the program was active in 47 states, with more than 19,000 certified tree farms comprising over 54 million acres. Orin Meyer (right) had his 10-acre woodland in Calumet County certified as a tree farm, one of 287 in Wisconsin in 1961.

By 1955, Wisconsin had a total of 2,175,748 acres in county forests in 27 counties. The forests produced more than $300,000 annually from timber sales during this time. Most of it came from natural growth, but the older plantations, like this one in the Oneida County Forest, already yielded some income from thinnings.

preparing management plans, giving planting advice, marking timber for harvest, improving timber stands, providing marketing assistance, and other related work.[9]

FORESTS PROVIDE ECONOMIC AND RECREATIONAL BENEFITS

Another trend after World War II was the increasing use of the national forests for pulpwood and sawtimber. The Sustained-Yield Forest Management Act of 1944, which authorized the creation of cooperative sustained-yield units with private industry in the national forests to maintain community stability, facilitated this trend. In 1949, the Nicolet National Forest had timber sales of 13.6 million board feet with a value of $155,000, and the Chequamegon National Forest totaled 16 million board feet worth $102,000. In 1951, the Nicolet forest produced 1,178,000 board feet of sawtimber, 22,376 cords of pulpwood, and a considerable volume of other forest products (telephone poles, fence posts, Christmas trees, etc.) worth $100,076. In 1952, the Chequamegon National Forest produced 38 million board feet of sawtimber and pulpwood.[10]

As the *Wisconsin Conservation Bulletin* noted in 1953, "Even now the Chequamegon forest is an economic asset to the North, furnishing employment to loggers and material for wood-using industries. It will become a . . . more important economic factor in the future, as more timber matures and as the quality improves."[11]

By 1953, the Chequamegon and Nicolet National Forests returned about $400,000 annually to the U.S. Treasury, 25 percent of which went to local governments and schools in lieu of taxes.[12]

Similarly, the county forests began to produce notable quantities of pulpwood and sawtimber. Marinette County provided a good example. The county set up a tightly controlled competitive system for stumpage bidding and inventoried all tracts before putting them up for sale. Stumpage sales totaled $22,000 in 1944, $26,000 in 1946, and almost $40,000 in 1950. At that time, the Marinette County Forest covered 223,800 acres. The county had 12,500 acres of pine plantation, and annual planting approached one million seedlings a year.[13]

By the late 1940s, the effects of the Forest Crop Law became increasingly apparent, especially in county forests. By 1949, 27 counties had more than two million acres of land entered under the Forest Crop Law, and the annual return from

timber harvests had reached more than $150,000. Besides timber production, these forests provided recreation, watershed protection, and wildlife habitat. The counties encouraged public use of the forests by establishing 57 improved parks and campsites. County forests also contained unimproved sites. The counties provided access to lakes and streams, established boat landings, and improved springs. Five dams were constructed, creating 3,100 acres of flowage that benefited waterfowl and furbearers.[14]

STATE FOREST MANAGEMENT IN THE 1950s

Following World War II, special emphasis on timber management, including timber sales, was given to the state forests. By 1955, state forests were beginning to see the same returns that county forests were experiencing. The seven state forests contained 276,385 acres. With approximately 20 years of satisfactory fire control, many acres had regrown to second-growth stands reaching merchantable size. These forests contained roughly 3,500 acres of mature timber, the largest area being located along the north fork of the Flambeau River.[15]

The Wisconsin Conservation Department

Between 1911 and 1955, state nurseries produced 443 million seedlings, with a peak output of 40 million in 1940. During the 1950s, 25 million trees were produced annually. The state sold about 60 percent of them to private landowners, with the remainder going to public lands. The photo shows the planting of white pine on private land in Oconto County.

operated tree nurseries at Wisconsin Rapids, Gordon, Trout Lake, Hayward, and Rhinelander in 1955. The department started a new nursery for game-management purposes, growing shrubs as well as trees at Boscobel.[16]

INSECTS AND DISEASE PROVE MORE HARMFUL

Despite advances in forestry management, forests still faced damage from insects and disease. In some years, insects and disease were more damaging than fire. As a result, in 1950 the Conservation Department added a forest entomologist to its staff and added two more in 1952. Shortly thereafter, the department hired a forest pathologist. In 1955, the passage of the Forest Pest Control Act gave the department power to aggressively suppress epidemic outbreaks of forest pests. In 1957, the department treated approximately 27,000 acres to control a serious outbreak of jack pine budworm and in 1958 treated more than 1,300 acres to control the Saratoga spittlebug.[17]

RESPONDING TO INCREASED DEMAND

By the end of World War II, many private forests had been overcut as a result of wartime demand for lumber and the postwar building boom. Demand for forest products of every description skyrocketed, and dozens of new logging and sawmill companies appeared. Many were short-term undertakings out to make a quick profit and had no interest in the future of the forest. Many woodland owners unknowingly sold choice stumpage at less than its value. Although there had been some forest management of industrial holdings earlier, it was at this point that many of the large forest-industry companies embarked on long-term management.[18]

LEADING THE COUNTRY

Nine Wisconsin companies—Nekoosa-Edwards Paper Company, National Container Corporation, Consolidated Water Power & Paper Company, Mosinee Paper Mills, Rhinelander Paper Company, Wisconsin Realty Company (Flambeau Paper Company), Goodman Lumber Company, Tigerton Lumber Company, and Holt Lumber Company—had certified industrial forests in 1950, totaling 544,512 acres. More than 40 million trees had been planted on these lands to that date. According to Hardy L. Shirley of the College of Forestry, Syracuse University, these forests were "some of the best and most intensively

Like a number of Wisconsin paper companies, Nekoosa-Edwards established a tree nursery as part of its reforestation program. Its highly mechanized operation reduced planting costs by 50 percent and increased seedling survival.

CONSOLIDATED'S EXPERIMENTAL FOREST[2]

During the 1930s, the Consolidated Water Power & Paper Company (now Stora Enso North America) began an acquisition program. By 1955, the company had accumulated 220,000 acres in the three lake states. To learn how to best manage stands for maximum pulpwood yield, the company established an experimental forest. Because the Lake States Forest Experiment Station and university research stations had already gathered data on the silvicultural characteristics of the region's mixed forests, the company began an experimental forest for the application of these findings rather than as a basic research center.

In 1948, the company established the Gagen Forest Management Unit, an area of 2,032 acres in eastern Oneida County, a tract typical of the 90,000 acres of the firm's timberlands within 25 miles of the unit. While small enough for economic and efficient management, it also proved large enough to serve as a model for the conditions common to the operation of an extensive industrial property. Through this pilot unit, the company sought to determine the kind of management that was feasible under various growth conditions, species distribution, and logging methods. Economics governed the degree of management, too. The company tested utilization practices so that it would not, for example, incur a cost of $100 to grow a unit area of pulpwood and then harvest only $80 worth of pulpwood from it.

managed forests in the country."[19]

In Wisconsin by the mid-1950s, close to three-quarters of a million acres were owned by industry and managed for permanent tree growth under standards approved by the Wisconsin Conservation Department. The companies planted more than 50 million trees on those acres needing reforestation, and two of the companies had their own nurseries. Four companies practiced selective cutting on stands of northern hardwoods. Pulp and paper mills owned more than 80 percent of this acreage. The companies made substantial investments in forest-fire detection and suppression equipment, which naturally supplemented state equipment for emergency purposes.[20]

The industrial forests became very important for recreation, particularly hunting, because the lands were open for public use.

By 1960, the 14 companies with industrial forests owned more than one million acres on which 64 million trees had been planted. They employed 57 foresters who worked in nearly all phases of forestry and timber production, from cruising and scaling to managing timberland divisions and acting as company officers. Industry had become a responsible and important part of Wisconsin's forestry community.[21]

THANKS to the vision and hard work of many people—and the resiliency of nature—Wisconsin's forests have recovered from the lumbering era when Europeans settled in the region. Today forests cover nearly half the state and provide countless public and private benefits. Wisconsin is once again blessed with a diverse and valuable resource that we depend on daily to meet a range of social, ecological, and economic needs. This color insert provides an overview of the 16-million-acre forest resource in Wisconsin today and the many ways the forest affects our lives every day—and how our lives, decisions, and actions affect the forest.

The investments of private landowners over the past 100 years have been key to reestablishing the rich forest resource of Wisconsin. The 260,000-plus individuals and families who own nearly 60 percent of the forestland in Wisconsin are a integral part of the success of sustainable forestry today—in partnership with the professional foresters who worked hard to rebuild the forest.

Elected leaders played a critical role in encouraging the rebirth of the forest resource by establishing programs to relieve tax pressures on private forest landowners; begin state, county, and school forests; and provide stable funding for the long-term stewardship of the forest. Today's leaders continue to play an important role in sustainable forest management.

The benefits of urban forests are often taken for granted. Trees do more than just provide beauty in a community. They release oxygen, absorb and trap carbon dioxide, slow storm runoff, furnish cooling shade in the summer and insulation in the winter, and provide homes for a variety of wildlife. Urban forests are vital to the health of the community.

NORTHERN HARDWOOD FORESTS

Left: Each type of forest requires a different type of management to maintain the tree species. Most forest regeneration in Wisconsin occurs naturally. Uneven-aged management practices can be used in northern hardwood forests because species such as sugar maple, yellow birch, and basswood are shade tolerant, meaning they can reproduce without full sunlight.

Left: Maintaining large blocks of forest habitat for songbirds, such as the yellow warbler, and other wildlife is increasingly difficult because of development pressures. A federal government program called Forest Legacy is helping with this issue through funding to acquire development and access rights on large blocks of private forestland.

Above: Beautiful spring flowers, such as trillium, pushing through the thick leaf litter of the forest floor signal the annual awakening of the North Woods.

Left: Forests are susceptible to pollution, insects, disease, and age. Native pests such as the forest tent caterpillar have cyclical outbreaks that create major havoc for people in the forests. Generally, the forest is resilient to these pests with help from natural predators or integrated pest management assistance from foresters.

Opposite page: Maple, basswood, green ash, and white ash are the most typical species in the northern hardwood forests. Sugar maple, Wisconsin's state tree, is economically important to Wisconsin for the thousands of visitors who travel to the forest to enjoy the autumn color pageant, for the sap that ranks Wisconsin among the top maple syrup producers, and for its beautiful wood used in many products.

WDNR

Opposite page: Although early succession forest types, like aspen and birch, are more common now than in the 1850s, they have been decreasing since the 1930s as the forests of Wisconsin age and succeed to more shade-tolerant species.

Left: Many of the state's most important game animals favor the aspen-birch forest.

JMAR FOTO-WERKS/WDNR

THOMAS A. MEYER/WDNR

JOHN ZASADA

Above: Special techniques for harvesting birch bark were used by Native Americans to prevent killing the birch trees. The bark was used for canoes, eating utensils, containers for cooking and storing, mats, baskets, snowshoes, and other uses.

Above left: Wild geranium is one of many plants in the Forest Habitat Type Classification System that Wisconsin foresters use to interpret the ecological potential of various forest sites.

ROBERT QUEEN/WDNR

Above: Aspen regenerates naturally after severe disturbances, either by sprouting after clear-cutting or seeding after fire. These disturbances—either natural or human caused—open up the forest canopy and allow sufficient light to penetrate to this sun-loving species.

Left: Aspen is very important to the pulp and paper industry. Wisconsin has been the top paper-producing state for the past 50 years. Pulp, paper, and allied firms employ more than 52,000 Wisconsin workers. The value of shipments from Wisconsin's paper companies tops $12.4 billion annually.

RICHARD HAMILTON SMITH

JMAR FOTO-WERKS

Opposite page: While oaks range from southern to northern Wisconsin in several habitat types, the oak-hickory forest type is at home in southern Wisconsin. Red and white oaks are the most harvested of Wisconsin's southern species. Wisconsin's hickories provide the hardest, most resilient wood of all the state's timber species.

Left: There are more than 1,800 forest-products companies in Wisconsin. A sampling of the wood products produced includes hardwood floors, pool cues, lumber, logs for homes, and fine hardwood furniture and cabinetry.

Left: Oak-hickory forests are havens for "nut-loving" wildlife. Squirrels, chipmunks, foxes, rabbits, mice, mallards, wood ducks, bobwhites, and wild turkeys are among the many species that eat hickory nuts and acorns from oak trees. The wild turkey was reintroduced to Wisconsin in 1976 and now inhabits almost three-quarters of the state.

WDNR

S. KELLY KEARNS/WDNR

Left: Invasive exotic species such as garlic mustard may be the greatest threat facing Wisconsin's rural and urban forests in the future. In addition to hampering outdoor recreational activities, invasive species also take an economic and ecological toll on Wisconsin's natural resources. Gypsy moth, buckthorn, and garlic mustard are among the exotic invasive species currently displacing native species and affecting citizens' livelihoods and quality of life.

DARRELL ZASTROW/WDNR

ROBERT QUEEN/WDNR

Left: Wild berries in Wisconsin's forests provide good food not only for wildlife but also for humans who enjoy berry picking as a recreational activity.

WDNR

Left: Much of Wisconsin's red pine resource is in plantations. This has been a commonly planted species from the 1930s, when Civilian Conservation Corps crews replanted on worn-out, nutrient-poor, sandy soils to prevent erosion and help recover the soil. While plantations make up less than 5 percent of Wisconsin's forests, they play an important role in fiber production, and red pine is important to the pulp and paper industry as well as for lumber and other uses.

ROBERT QUEEN/WDNR

Above: During the lumbering era, nearly all large white pines were harvested. Now white pine is making a comeback as a result of natural regeneration as well as planting. Along with the bald eagle, white pine is once again an important part of Wisconsin's landscape.

Opposite page: Eastern white pine, red pine, and jack pine are the common pine species in Wisconsin. The white pine is Wisconsin's largest conifer. The large size, straight trunk, and high fiber content have made white pine valuable historically and today.

RICHARD HAMILTON SMITH

WDNR

WDNR

Left: The proliferation of homes within Wisconsin's forests poses a tremendous fire danger, and ecological and economic concerns through fragmentation of the forest.

Below left: Since the first Earth Day in 1970, the average family size in the United States has dropped by 16 percent, while the size of the average single-family house being built has increased by 48 percent. Today the U.S. public consumes more resources, including wood and wood products, than at any time in its history and more per capita than almost every other nation.

HERBERT LANGE/WDNR

ROBERT QUEEN/WDNR

Far left: Many creatures great and small, such as the black bear, call the spruce-fir forest home.

Left: Balsam fir, Fraser fir, Scotch pine, and white spruce are among the species grown in Wisconsin for Christmas trees. A leading producer of Christmas trees, Wisconsin annually harvests more than three million of the holiday evergreens in addition to many tons of boughs for decorations. There are some 65,000 acres of commercial Christmas trees on more than 100 farms throughout the state.

WISCONSIN DEPARTMENT OF TOURISM

Left: Many Wisconsin residents enjoy winter sports such as cross-country skiing and snowmobiling. The level and range of recreational demands on Wisconsin forests continue to grow.

ROBERT QUEEN/WDNR

Left: On lands protected by the DNR, approximately 1,500 fires burn over 5,000 acres annually. More than 90 percent of these fires are human caused, with debris burning the leading cause. The wildfire program depends on the citizens of the state to act responsibly in the forest to prevent fires and to report fires so DNR forestry personnel can suppress the fires as quickly as possible. A limited number of fire towers are staffed during the fire season.

USDA FOREST SERVICE

Opposite page: The spruce-fir forest is the most common forest type in northern Wisconsin. These forests are typically very diverse and can be found on dry or moist sites. They often surround and blend into bogs. Important tree species in this forest type include white spruce, black spruce, balsam fir, tamarack, quaking aspen, and white pine.

ROBERT QUEEN/WDNR

Left: One of the primary reasons for establishing forest reserves in the early 1900s was to protect the headwaters of Wisconsin rivers in the northern counties. In addition to their important ecological values, Wisconsin's forested water resources are important for aesthetic and recreational values.

JMAR FOTO-WERKS/WDNR

WDNR

Left: Timber wolves have returned to Wisconsin forests, and the population is increasing. Wolves are important top predators in our forests.

Left: The number of undeveloped lakes in Wisconsin is declining with increasing development along forested shorelines.

Left: Over 5,000 products that we use in our daily lives are made from wood or wood by-products. The forest products industry in Wisconsin directly employs nearly 100,000 people.

ROBERT QUEEN/WDNR

Opposite page: Wisconsin has 1.5 million acres classified as bottomland hardwood forests. Primary species in this forest type are soft maple (such as silver and red maple), elm, and black ash.

THOMAS A. MEYER/WDNR

WDNR

Opposite page: The swamp conifer forest type, consisting of tamarack, black spruce, and white cedar, accounts for about 6 percent of Wisconsin forestland. White cedar is the longest-lived tree in Wisconsin.

Left: Wisconsin's forests determine the quality and quantity of the water released into nearby lakes, streams, and drinking-water supplies. Today's forest management practices minimize soil disturbances and prevent debris from washing into water bodies.

THOMAS A. MEYER/WDNR

WDNR

Left: A wide range of nontimber forest products is harvested in Wisconsin, including sphagnum moss in the Black River State Forest. Other specialty products include morel mushrooms and balsam fir boughs.

Far left: Tamarack is the only conifer in Wisconsin to turn golden and shed its needles every fall.

THOMAS A. MEYER/WDNR

Above: Many rare species such as the calypso orchid are at home in swamp conifer forests.

TODAY'S FORESTRY PROFESSIONALS are dedicated to the protection and sustainable management of Wisconsin's forests. As the forestry profession in Wisconsin moves into its second hundred years, our forests once again offer a wide range of social, ecological, and economic benefits. Through ongoing, collaborative commitment by professionals and citizens, we can ensure that these benefits will be available for future generations.

WDNR

DARRELL ZASTROW/WDNR

ROBERT QUEEN/WDNR

TREES FOR TOMORROW STEPS UP EFFORTS

Like industrial forestry, the work of Trees For Tomorrow greatly increased in the post–World War II period. Between 1944 and 1949, Trees For Tomorrow distributed two million seedlings to private timberland owners. Its staff checked the planting sites and made survival counts to ensure the best results. Between 1946 and 1949, it mapped 25,000 acres of private woodlands and developed management plans for them.[22]

To provide conservation education, Trees For Tomorrow began a conservation camp (now Resources Education Center) at Eagle River. In 1947, 1,265 people from 67 Wisconsin counties and 42 states registered at the camp. Trees For Tomorrow has worked with the U.S. Forest Service, the Wisconsin Conservation Department (later the Department of Natural Resources), the UW–Extension, and various colleges and universities to educate teachers and students about conservation through field institutes and seminars.[23]

CONSULTING BECOMES IMPORTANT TO CONTINUED SUCCESS

As industrial forestry matured in the

By the 1960s, more than 1,400 students from over 100 high schools had attended the Trees For Tomorrow summer camp each year. Individuals and civic and service organizations sponsored most of the students through fellowships or grants.

post–World War II period, so did the field of forestry consulting. After fire destroyed its sawmill in 1949, George Banzhaf & Company restricted its operations to forestry consulting. In the 1950s, on the basis of several studies for the rapidly expanding pulp and paper industry, the company firmly established itself as a leader in timber-supply analysis, advising clients throughout the country on the feasibility of new processing capacity. Over the course of its existence, the company has served most of the major forest products corporations in North America as well as public agencies, investment banks, attorneys, and insurance companies.[24]

REMARKABLE PROGRESS SEEN AT MIDCENTURY

In 1905, Wisconsin produced 390,000 cords of pulpwood, and some experts expected the state to run out of pulpwood by 1920. In 1946, the state supplied 428,000 cords. Only reforestation and forest management by the federal government, the state, individual counties, private landowners, and private industry made this possible. In 1949 alone almost 20 million trees were planted in Wisconsin.[25]

Despite such progress, more remained to be accomplished. So in 1953, the Wisconsin Chamber of Commerce, in cooperation with 57 organizations in the state, sponsored the Wisconsin Silver Anniversary Forestry Conference at Milwaukee.[26]

At the conference, D. C. Everest of the Marathon Paper Mills Company expressed the opinion, "Our objective in forestry is to develop to the fullest extent possible, the timber producing potential of Wisconsin's forestlands in the shortest practical time, while at the same time giving consideration to the other commercial and non-commercial purposes which forests serve."[27]

To meet this objective, meeting participants suggested that Wisconsin create a state program with federal and industrial input for insect and disease control. Further, participants suggested continuous research, especially in the fields of entomology, pathology, and genetics; forest management, particularly on public forests, that would consider water and soil conservation, recreation, and wildlife; more effective fire control and expansion of fire protection to all parts of the state; an accurate and reasonably current forest inventory; and education of the public about the importance of forest management.[28]

The conference participants suggested more widespread forest management on all timberlands, but especially on farmlands and small woodlands.

They recommended the formation of an organization of woodland owners interested in pursuing the common goals and objectives associated with their ownership of forestland. This organization eventually became the Wisconsin Woodland Owners Association Inc.[29]

PRESERVING NATURAL AREAS

By the 1940s, Wisconsin citizens had long expressed concern for the loss of their native vegetation. In 1945 the State Conservation Commission, on a motion by Aldo Leopold, established a Natural Areas Committee to begin the process of acquiring botanical areas of particular value, by gift or purchase. It had a budget of $5,000 for the 1945–1946 fiscal year and consisted of F. G. Wilson from the Wisconsin Conservation Department, Norman Fassett from the University of Wisconsin, and Albert Fuller from the Milwaukee Public Museum. The first two natural areas the state acquired were Parfrey's Glen (Sauk County) and the Cedarburg Bog (Ozaukee County).[30]

In 1950, State Forester C. L. Harrington determined that the most appropriate use for natural areas was scientific study and that the state needed a permanent committee of scientists to provide advice on how to preserve and manage these areas. Wisconsin Statute 23.27 established the State Board for the Preservation of Scientific Areas (now called the Natural Areas Preservation Council [NAPC]) in 1951 and initiated the first state natural area preservation program in the country. John Curtis served as its first chair and championed the idea of using and studying the natural processes in vegetation, especially forests, as a means of guiding conservation. By December 1952, the board had designated 16 natural areas, and by spring 1961 the number had increased to 32.[31]

In 1950, the Ecologists' Union began to call for a national system of natural area preserves, which gave rise to The Nature Conservancy in 1951. The group's goal was and continues to be to preserve plants, animals, and natural communities that represent diversity by protecting the lands and waters they need to survive. The Wisconsin chapter of The Nature Conservancy began in the spring of 1960. Its first project was Abraham's Woods in Green County, a 40-acre remnant of a climax or terminal forest and dry prairie combination representing the landscape of pre- and early settlement Wisconsin. The conservancy transferred the preserve to the University of

Wisconsin, and it now serves as a teaching and research laboratory.[32]

FROM CUTOVER TO GREENERY

By 1960, Wisconsin had one of the most effective forest-conservation services in the United States. It could point with pride to its forest-tax laws, which allowed private investors to engage profitably in the growing of new forests. Its two million acres of county forests, which had been created under a cooperative arrangement between counties and the state, was unique in this country. Wisconsin pioneered forest-recreational zoning.

Although the public may soon forget the men and women who fashioned this transformation, today's forests serve as their living legacy.

With the return of the forest, differing views on how to manage and use it developed and led to more challenges in Wisconsin's forest history.[33]

These views show forest succession along Vilas County Road M between 1911 and the 1990s at what is now called Landmark Pines. The tall pines on the right side of each photo are the same trees, having witnessed the regeneration of the forest for nearly 100 years. (Opposite) In 1911, a rutted, mud wagon trail cuts through a burned-over young forest. (Top left) By the 1930s, the regenerating forest is dominated by sun-loving aspen. (Top right) In the 1950s, pine begins to take over the previously aspen-dominated location. (Bottom left) In the 1970s, pine has replaced aspen. (Bottom right) And in the 1990s, pines have continued to grow and prosper.

75

CHAPTER SIX

CHANGING VIEWS ON FOREST USE (1960–2004)
THE ROAD FROM SUSTAINED YIELD TO SUSTAINABLE FORESTRY

"NOT SO LONG AGO, *northern Wisconsin was described as an area of utter devastation—a region of stump prairies.*
Today the forests are green again." —Erling Solberg, Agricultural Economist with the Farm Economics Research Division, 1961

If there was one constant during the 1960s and 1970s, it was change. Where earlier the emphasis was on intensive timber harvest and then sustained yield, during these decades forestry gradually moved in the direction of sustainable forestry, which balances the social, ecological, and economic values of the forest.

The change began in 1960, when President Eisenhower signed the Multiple Use–Sustained Yield Act, which specified that national forests be administered for outdoor recreation, range, timber, watershed, and wildlife and fish purposes in ways that best served the public's needs. An important clause, and one that is still pointed to as the first requirement for sustainability, states, "Without impairment of the productivity of the land." This idea not only guided management of national forests but also influenced management of state and county forests, as well as private woodlands.

In the 1960s, conservation and recreation interest groups, including the Audubon Society, Izaak Walton League, the Sierra Club, and the Wilderness Society, moved into the political arena. They put concern for the quality of the

Protection of water quality became an important issue for the forestry community in the 1960s.

A section of the Flambeau River flows through the Flambeau River State Forest in northern Wisconsin.

environment on the political agenda and created public will for change. During this time, Congress passed the Land and Water Conservation Fund Act (1964), the Wilderness Act (1964), and the National Scenic and Wild Rivers and National Trails System Acts (1968).

With these landmark pieces of legislation in place, the stage was set for the development of both public and private initiatives to preserve, improve, and expand Wisconsin forests. Changes instituted included new management practices for county forests (the largest government-owned forests in the state), the reorganization of the Wisconsin Conservation Department, and additional financial assistance for private landowners.

WISCONSIN COUNTY FORESTS ASSOCIATION

As a result of amendments to the Forest Crop Law in the late 1950s, counties began to question their partnership with the state and wondered whether they might be better off discontinuing their participation in the county forest program. Representatives from 22 counties met in Phillips, Wisconsin, on December 6, 1960, to fight for revisions to this law. They created a Wisconsin County Forests Executive Committee

to present initiatives to the state legislature. This led to the enactment, on September 19, 1963, of the County Forest Law, which made the program permanent. It changed the program's emphasis from tax relief and land rehabilitation to development and management for optimum production of forest products, while ensuring maximum public benefits via multiple uses.

In 1968, the Wisconsin County Forests Association Inc. (WCFA) was established to provide a forum to consider problems, programs, and policies of the county forests. Members consisted of county board officials, who served on their respective county forestry committees. Today, all 29 county forests are members of the association. Since its formation, the WCFA has provided leadership and counsel related to county forestry policies and programs. The WCFA works with private groups and public agencies to strengthen forestry and forest-related programs in the state.

The 2.3 million acres of county forestland statewide are jointly administered by the respective counties and the Wisconsin Department of Natural Resources (DNR, previously the Wisconsin Conservation Department). The counties own the land and provide administration and supervision through county forest administrators. These

administrators report to the county boards and have direct supervision of the land through county forestry committees. The county boards establish policies and procedures regulating all the activities that take place in county forests. County forest administrators and their staff direct the day-to-day operations of the forests and serve as the main point of contact with the DNR.

The DNR assigns a liaison forester to each county forest to provide technical advice and on-the-ground assistance. The state provides financial assistance to the counties to develop and enhance the forests. In addition, the state makes an annual payment in lieu of taxes to the towns in which the county forests are located.

By the early 1980s, sales of forest products from Wisconsin's county forests approached $3 million annually. By 1995, revenues exceeded $9 million annually. The bulk of these funds (more than 70 percent) is retained by the counties for county forest and general operations. A small portion goes to the state to repay county forest loans that may be outstanding. And a minimum of 10 percent of the timber sale revenue goes to the towns in which the county forests are located. In addition to this economic impact, these forests provide habitat for wildlife and recreational opportunities for thousands of people.

WISCONSIN DEPARTMENT OF NATURAL RESOURCES FORMED

In 1967, the Kellet Reorganization Act consolidated the state's Conservation and Resource Development Departments, along with several small agencies, into a single resource management agency: the Wisconsin Department of Natural Resources. The organization combined traditional conservation management and newer environmental responsibilities, such as regulation of air and water pollution, solid waste disposal, and shoreland protection. The change generated much concern that traditional conservation programs would lose importance to environmental programs in the new bureaucracy, prompting sportsmen to march in a "red-shirt rally" around the State Capitol. The DNR was divided into six divisions: Forestry, Wildlife, and Recreation; Environmental Protection; Enforcement; Tourism; Trust Lands and Investments; and General Services.

The act created a part-time, nonpaid, citizen policymaking board, the Natural Resources Board, whose seven members serve six-year terms. It also kept intact the segregated conservation fund and

continued the Wisconsin Conservation Congress and other advisory bodies.

ENVIRONMENTAL ISSUES MOVE TO THE FOREFRONT

The early stages of the environmental movement, from the publication of *Silent Spring* by Rachel Carson in 1962, to the first Earth Day, focused attention on species and natural resources that previously had been overlooked.

The first Earth Day was held on April 22, 1970. Earth Day was the brainchild of Gaylord Nelson, U.S. senator from Wisconsin, who wanted to "inspire a public demonstration so big it would shake the political establishment out of its lethargy and force the environmental issue onto the national political agenda."[1] The man who had previously served as the state's governor, and was referred to as Wisconsin's "conservation governor," did just that. Thousands of Wisconsin citizens and millions of Americans took part in nationwide tree plantings, meetings, debates, demonstrations, and teach-ins. Conservation and environmental groups, some comparatively new and some long-standing ones, quickly capitalized on this public awareness, pushing the cause of environmental protection through the news media and lobbying legislative

During the early 1960s, Wisconsin was a leader in the national movement of environmental reform promoted by Governor (and later Senator) Gaylord Nelson. In 1969, Nelson launched a speaking tour emphasizing conservation issues. He called on citizens to meet in "teach-ins" to discuss the "imminent crisis of the environment." The result was Earth Day, April 22, 1970, now considered a milestone in American environmentalism.

Urban foresters care for trees to maximize their survivability, especially in times of extreme weather conditions, such as a drought. This crew waters newly planted trees during the drought of 1988.

bodies at the local, state, and national levels.

URBAN FORESTRY

As Wisconsin moved from a rural to an urban society, the need for green spaces, parks, and trees within cities was recognized as a quality-of-life issue and led to the development of urban forestry. Typically, more than half of every community's trees are on public property—along streets, in parks and playgrounds, along recreational trails, around businesses, and in open spaces. Urban forestry, the scientific management of vegetation under urban conditions, focuses primarily on caring for individual trees and developing the urban forest for the enjoyment and benefit of the community.

In addition to their value for wildlife habitat, air quality, and conservation of soil and water, urban forests provide social and environmental benefits. They make parks and walkways more attractive and contribute to improved mental health and increased property values in urban neighborhoods. Urban forests conserve energy by mitigating heat in summer and insulating in winter.

About 4.7 percent of Wisconsin's total land area—about 1.7 million acres—is urban forest. Some of the trees in an urban forest may be native remnants preserved during development, but usually they are deliberately planted. Species range from naturally occurring Wisconsin natives to cultivated varieties of native species (cultivars) and exotic species from other parts of the world. Because urban forests surround them daily, many Wisconsin residents are more familiar with the tree varieties in a city setting than in the forest.

One approach to encouraging communities to invest in and care for urban trees is the Tree City USA (TCUSA) program. The program began when Nebraska's Division of Tourism celebrated its centennial Arbor Day in 1972; it became national in 1976 with events in 42 communities. By 2002, there were more than 2,800 Tree Cities across the country. (Wisconsin has 143 Tree Cities, ranking it third in the nation.) A community applying for Tree City recognition must have a tree board or commission with legal responsibility for the community's public trees. The board must establish tree ordinances and review long-term plans to remove dead and diseased trees, replace old trees with disease-resistant varieties, and plant and maintain trees. Tree Cities must also have community forestry budgets of at least $2 per capita and hold officially proclaimed Arbor Day observances.

In 1990, Congress passed a farm bill that authorized federal urban forestry assistance to states.

Within a year, the Wisconsin DNR had hired a state urban forestry coordinator, and the legislature amended state statutes to establish a state urban forestry grant program, which began in 1993. In 1992, the first State Urban Forestry Conference met, and the secretary of the DNR appointed an Urban Forestry Council. At that time, Milwaukee's urban forestry program, the largest in the state, employed a full-time staff of 184 and had an annual budget that exceeded $10 million. Since 1991, when the DNR began assisting communities with the building of sustainable tree-care programs, the number of Wisconsin communities providing management for their trees has more than doubled, from 106 to 266.

INVENTORY OF THREATENED SPECIES AND NATURAL COMMUNITIES

With the environmental movement came a belief that wild or wilderness areas needed to be protected and preserved to study and reflect on the balance of nature. In October 1973, the Natural Resources Board adopted a resolution that led to the appointment of a Wild Resources Advisory Council to help establish wild and wilderness areas as well as wild rivers and lakes. This resulted in

WAUKESHA: A CASE STUDY OF URBAN FORESTRY

Waukesha has been a pioneer in urban forestry, and because of the city's commitment to its natural resources, Waukesha's trees live an average of 35–50 years—much longer than the national average.

Urban forestry has been practiced in Waukesha since the mid-1950s. In the mid-1960s, the city started a formal program with the hiring of full-time professional foresters to battle Dutch elm disease. In 1976, city ordinances designated the Parks and Recreation Board responsible for the community's trees. Waukesha has been a Tree City since 1979.

Waukesha's forestry program includes planning and designing public landscapes in new areas, replacing plantings in established neighborhoods, and maintaining the community's investment in trees. Ten arborists manage nearly 30,000 street trees and 7,000 to 10,000 public trees on nearly 800 acres of parklands, wetlands, and other public spaces. Arborists also operate a small municipal nursery that grows lindens, Norway maples, flowering crab trees, and flowering pear trees. A computer inventory keeps an up-to-date census of tree locations, species planted, size, health, maintenance history, and approximate value. Waukesha uses about 20 different species as street trees, which are strong-wooded, wide-branched trees that will not be messy, a street nuisance, or a traffic hazard.

Calypso bulbosa **is one of many plants at risk that is found in Wisconsin. It is listed on the Natural Heritage Inventory System.**

the creation of wilderness areas, wild lakes, and several new wild rivers in Wisconsin, mostly under state ownership.

In the 1970s, The Nature Conservancy (TNC) developed an international network of inventory programs to compare sites and elements of natural diversity. TNC focused its protection efforts on the most threatened species and communities. In 1985, TNC entered into a cooperative venture with the Wisconsin DNR to establish a Natural Heritage Inventory System, an ongoing inventory of plants, animals, and natural communities that are at risk on a statewide or national basis. This inventory helps guide the DNR and others in the management of Wisconsin's forests.

TRIBAL TREATY RIGHTS

In March 1974, when two members of the Lac Courte Oreilles Band of Lake Superior Chippewa Indians were cited for spearing fish, public forests were involved in a 17-year-long legal battle. The Lac Courte Oreilles Band filed a class-action lawsuit on behalf of the two tribal fishermen, arguing that the state of Wisconsin was depriving the tribes of their rights reserved in the treaties of 1837 and 1842. Those rights included

hunting, fishing, and gathering on off-reservation lands within the ceded territory now encompassed by the northern third of Wisconsin. From 1978 through the late 1980s, a number of decisions were rendered in the litigation; some of these decisions were later overturned.

By the late 1980s, the gathering-rights issue rose to the forefront. The lawsuit initially focused on hunting and fishing rights off reservation land, which was more of a statewide issue. However, inclusion of timber harvesting into the gathering-rights issue raised the level of interest among private landowners, counties, and towns in which timber production and the forest-products industry were important to their economies.

In 1991, after 17 years, federal judge Barbara Crabb entered the final judgment in the lawsuit filed against the state by six Chippewa bands. The decision let stand federal rulings that granted the Chippewa rights to gather miscellaneous forest products, hunt deer, and spearfish off-reservation lands in northern Wisconsin that were ceded in the treaties of 1837 and 1842. Among the key points stipulated in the decision, those relative to forestry included clarification that the treaties do not extend to the commercial harvest of timber; the state has the ultimate authority to protect and manage the resources in the ceded territory; and tribal members cannot enter onto privately owned lands to exercise their rights. Today, state and county forests and the waters of the state continue to provide for fishing, hunting, and gathering as provided for in that decision.[2]

WATER QUALITY ACT

The 1977 Clean Water Act required each state to develop plans and procedures to control silviculturally related nonpoint sources of pollution. Ten years later, the Water Quality Act required each state to reduce nonpoint source pollution to the maximum extent possible. Working in partnership with government and industry, environmental organizations, and recreational interests, the Wisconsin DNR developed forestry Best Management Practices (BMPs) for Water Quality. Wisconsin BMPs provide voluntary guidelines to landowners, loggers, and land managers for protecting water quality. The most practical and cost-effective method to ensure that forestry operations do not adversely affect water quality is through the use of these voluntary BMPs.

Public and private landowners in Wisconsin use forestry BMPs to guide their management activities. For example, compliance is required

To protect the beauty and purity of Wisconsin's waters, the DNR has implemented Best Management Practices for Water Quality to guide landowners in the state. Studies have shown that the voluntary guidelines are effective 99 percent of the time when applied correctly.

HELPING THE KARNER BLUE BUTTERFLY

Wisconsin supports the largest population of the endangered Karner blue butterfly of any location in the world. The habitat conservation plan developed in Wisconsin to protect the Karner blue butterfly habitat has been very successful.

The U.S. Fish & Wildlife Service listed the Karner blue butterfly, as an endangered species in 1992. The caterpillar depends on wild lupine growing in young forests, barrens, savannas, and prairies as its primary source of food. Many of these areas are threatened by development, agriculture, roadside management, and succession of the land from fields to shrubby woodland. Wisconsin has the most widespread populations along with Indiana, Michigan, Minnesota, New Hampshire, and New York. But Karner blue population numbers have dropped in the United States because the habitat where wild lupine grows has been developed or divided up for roads, buildings, towns, and cities.

Following a multiyear effort, a statewide habitat conservation plan was adopted in 1999. To date, 37 major land managers, including representatives from the forest industry, utilities, government agencies, and roadway-management authorities, participate in the habitat conservation plan. This agreement allows Wisconsin land managers to continue operating in and around Karner blue habitat, provided they modify their activities to minimize harm to Karner blues. The partnership works in cooperation with countless volunteer groups, landowner coalitions, and concerned citizens across a vast area of the state to incorporate Karner blue considerations into land management decisions.

Through these combined efforts, more than 260,000 acres have been designated to help ensure the Karner blue butterfly's continued survival.

84

on DNR properties, such as state forests, and is integrated into management plans for private lands enrolled in the Managed Forest Law program. Additionally, all 29 counties enrolled in Wisconsin's County Forest Law program have adopted forestry BMPs for Water Quality. And much of Wisconsin's industrial forestland is enrolled in the American Forest and Paper Association's Sustainable Forestry Initiative (SFI), which requires water-quality BMP compliance and logger training as a condition of membership.

Monitoring of randomly selected sales of timber harvested between 1994 and 1996 disclosed that 85 percent of the time, BMPs have been applied correctly and that, when applied correctly, BMPs were effective in protecting water quality in 99 percent of the cases. Further monitoring in 2002 yielded similar positive results.

FORESTRY AT THE UNIVERSITY LEVEL

Wisconsin could not become a national leader in forestry without expanding professionalism within the field, and this could only be accomplished through education and research. Although forestry classes at the University of Wisconsin–Madison date back to the early 1900s, it wasn't until 1934 that a

UW–Stevens Point professor Robert Rogers and a student conduct research in the field. UW–Stevens Point is recognized as having one of the top forestry programs in the country.

Sustainable forestry professor Ray Guries discusses timber management with forestry and environmental studies students during a field trip to the UW Arboretum. UW–Madison is a leader in forestry education and research.

program for professional foresters began.

In 1968, the Coordinating Council for Higher Education approved the University of Wisconsin–Madison and Wisconsin State University–Stevens Point (now the University of Wisconsin–Stevens Point) to offer majors in forestry. UW–Madison would teach forest science, and UW–Stevens Point would teach forest management. The Society of American Foresters gave full accreditation to the forestry programs at Madison in 1971 and Stevens Point in 1976. UW–Stevens Point received approval for a second degree emphasis in forest administration in 1971 and added an urban forestry emphasis in 1974 and a forest recreation emphasis in 1978. By 1981, the forestry program at UW–Stevens Point had become the largest in the nation and continues to be in 2004.

National Education Standards Inc. has consistently ranked UW–Madison's undergraduate program in forest science as one of the four best in the country. The UW–Madison Department of Forest Ecology and Management is the principal provider of forestry research and extension education within the University of Wisconsin system and the state. Not only have graduates of Wisconsin programs added to the knowledge and expertise of our state, but their influence has spread throughout the country and many foreign nations.

YOUTH CONSERVATION CORPS PROVES VERY SUCCESSFUL

Building on the Civilian Conservation Corps tradition, the state established the Youth Conservation Corps (YCC) in 1961; within the first nine months, almost 200 youth had enrolled. This program not only provided employment for young people but also provided for the completion of many important conservation projects.

Two-thirds of the nearly 80,000 worker days during the first five years of the program went into timber-stand improvement such as clearing, planting, thinning, and release projects, along with parks development. Initially, the YCC was administered cooperatively by the Public Welfare Department and the Wisconsin Conservation Department, but the 1967 Kellet Reorganization Act transferred sole responsibility for the YCC to the new DNR.

"The simple truth of the matter," said YCC chief Ray Hendrikse, "is that without the assistance of the youth camps, development, restoration and maintenance of state parks, wildlife areas, forests,

CONSERVATION AND FORESTRY HALLS OF FAME

As people became more cognizant of the environment and the need to judiciously use natural resources, they began to appreciate the efforts of early conservationists and environmentalists. Two outgrowths of this appreciation are the Wisconsin Conservation Hall of Fame and the Wisconsin Forestry Hall of Fame, both established in 1984 and located at UW–Stevens Point.

The individuals enshrined in the Conservation Hall of Fame have significantly contributed to conservation programs, projects, public understanding, and conservation ethics. They include foresters and other natural resource managers, writers, researchers, lawyers, and educators. The Conservation Hall of Fame includes an interactive museum displaying the progression of natural resource conservation in Wisconsin. A formal gallery commemorating the inductees is located at the Schmeeckle Reserve Visitor Center in Stevens Point.

Public and private forestry organizations established the Wisconsin Forestry Hall of Fame to recognize individuals who have contributed significantly to the practice and progress of forestry in Wisconsin. Inductees include foresters, conservation advocates, legislators, lumbermen, researchers, forest rangers, paper producers, and teachers. The Forestry Hall of Fame exhibit, which includes a plaque for each inductee, is housed in the UW–Stevens Point College of Natural Resources building. (A list of inductees can be found in the Appendix.)

streams, and lakes would be severely reduced. Without them, conservation work would continue to get done, but to a much lesser degree."

In the 1970s, the federal government established its own Youth Conservation Corps, modeled after Wisconsin's program. On August 13, 1970, President Richard Nixon established a three-year pilot summer employment program for youth ages 15 to 17. The main objective of the federal Youth Conservation Corps was to gainfully employ young people in a conservation, work-education program on public lands and waters under the administration of the Departments of Agriculture and the Interior.

The Youth Conservation Corps program proved so successful that Congress expanded it and made it a permanent national endeavor on September 3, 1974. The new legislation authorized $60 million annually for the federal Youth Conservation Corps.

In 1983, the state legislature established the Wisconsin Conservation Corps (WCC). Through June 30, 1995, the WCC employed more than 6,250 young adults in 515 projects throughout the state. The projects ranged from fish and wildlife improvement to state park and forest enhancement to community development. However, because

of budget cuts, WCC crew numbers dwindled from nearly 60 crews statewide to 20 in 2003, and the program was eliminated later that year.

THE WISCONSIN FOREST ACCORD, FIRST FOR THE NATION

With many entities at the state and federal levels affecting forestry decisions, it became apparent that land managers lacked a common language. This lack of common ecological language was a major barrier to communication and sharing information. The DNR and UW–Madison worked together to address the problem, and the Wisconsin Forest Accord evolved as a solution.

The Wisconsin Forest Accord is a memorandum of understanding to use a common language for forest resource management. It specifies using the Forest Habitat Type Classification System and the National Hierarchical Framework of Ecological Units (NHFEU). The Forest Habitat Type Classification System, an ecological tool, promotes a common language for interpreting site capability based on potential natural vegetation. It has been developed for Wisconsin and is applicable across all ownerships. The NHFEU divides landscapes into ecologically significant regions at multiple scales.

The Forest Habitat Type Classification System is the vegetative component of the NHFEU. In July 1994, more than a dozen public, industrial, and private landowners, land managers, and land-managing agencies signed on to the accord. It was the first time that an entire state had adopted uniform criteria to share ecological information between private landowners and county, state, and federal agencies.

ASSISTANCE AVAILABLE TO LANDOWNERS

In Wisconsin, 57 percent of forestland (nine million acres) is owned by individuals and families, and an additional 4 percent (700,000 acres) is owned by companies not involved in the forest-products industry. Together these are identified as nonindustrial private forest (NIPF) lands. These more than nine million acres are owned by approximately 260,000 different individuals or families. Excluding small tracts of less than 10 acres, the average private landowner owns about 55 acres of forestland.

More than 64 percent of the timber harvested in Wisconsin between 1983 and 1996 came off NIPF lands, making these tracts very significant to the state's economy. NIPF lands also provide critical

WISCONSIN'S FOREST INVENTORIES

Sustainably managing forests means knowing what resources are available. As a result, a series of Wisconsin forest inventories have been conducted listing and summarizing the quantity and quality of forest resources and assessing their use. The inventories were established after passage of two federal laws—the McSweeny-McNary Forest Research Act of 1928 and the Forest and Rangeland Renewable Resources Planning Act of 1974—which required the U.S. Forest Service to provide Congress with periodic assessments of forests and related resources on a national scale.

Wisconsin's first statewide inventory was completed under this system in 1936. It used aerial photos and check plots on the ground. The second Wisconsin inventory, in 1956, was a cooperative venture involving both public and private entities, including the Wisconsin Conservation Department, 32 northern counties, private companies, and the U.S. Forest Service North Central Forest Experiment Station.

In 1968, the third Wisconsin inventory incorporated a newly designed sampling system and computer model. The new system used the information gathered to simulate the germination, growth, harvest, and death of individual trees and made 30-year projections for Wisconsin's forests.

A fourth inventory conducted in 1983 was similar to the 1968 inventory, but the sample quantity was doubled. This survey determined the amount of Wisconsin timber used by state and out-of-state sawmills, pulp mills, and veneer mills. In addition, it developed estimates of fuel wood used by homeowners and industry. A fifth survey was conducted in 1996, using the same sampling methods, but the database was expanded and refined. In general, the inventory analyzes the area, species composition, and volume of the statewide forest resource. More detail has been incorporated on land ownerships, ecological information on habitat types, and forest health data regarding insects and disease. Likewise, the inventory determines changes in the forest resource, including those occurring naturally and those changes related to the level of management applied to the variety of forestlands.

Beginning in 2000, data have been collected annually to get more accurate, up-to-date information. As a result, foresters will be in Wisconsin's forests each year, measuring about 20 percent of the 1,900 plots in the state. The statewide inventory will be completed in five-year cycles. Specific plot-level information collected includes tree diameter, height, log length, and grade; tree health (damage, crown ratio, and crown position); site data (aspect, slope, and forest type); forest regeneration; shrubs and forbs; insects and disease; dead and down wood; and harvesting information.

Private consulting foresters assist landowners to most effectively and successfully manage their land. Consultants may inventory land, create management plans, and appraise land and timber, in addition to many other tasks.

wildlife habitat for a wide array of endangered and threatened species, as well as recreation and other noncommodity values.

The goal of the DNR private forestry program is to motivate landowners to practice sustainable forestry, provide technical assistance, and refer them to service providers who can help them accomplish forestry projects. This is a challenging task not only because of the large number of landowners but also because less than 20 percent of NIPF landowners have written forest-management plans. Further, in many southern and central counties, forestland is now more valuable than farmland. These increasing values are heightening the pressure to partition forestland into ever smaller parcels. Therefore, the number of NIPF landowners will continue to increase.

With the increase of both public and private forests and the desire by NIPF landowners to manage their land, the workloads of DNR foresters and demands for their assistance have steadily increased. This has affected the types and amounts of assistance DNR has offered to woodland owners and has increased opportunities in the field for private-sector consulting foresters, woodland organizations, and programs that provide assistance to woodland owners.

CONSULTANTS AID IN FOREST MANAGEMENT

A 1974 DNR survey showed that Wisconsin had 20 full-time and part-time private consulting foresters; by 1989, there were 39 private consulting firms. Consulting foresters offer landowners assistance in every phase of forestry, from appraisal of a single shade tree to an inventory of thousands of acres of forestland. Consultants also provide expert testimony in court cases, settle damage claims, set up and administer timber sales, appraise timber and land, and advise on enhancing forestland for wildlife, recreation, and aesthetics.

The Wisconsin Consulting Foresters Association was formed in 2002 to provide forestry services to landowners whose objective is to practice sustainable forestry. A major theme of the organization is to provide a high ethical standard of forest management. The association works collaboratively with the DNR, Wisconsin Woodland Owners Association, and the Society of American Foresters.

While the DNR still provides technical assistance, its role evolved into one emphasizing initial guidance, landowner motivation, financial incentives, and project facilitation as laid out in NR 1.21 of the Wisconsin Administrative Code.

The rule also authorized the Cooperating Forester Program in 1989. Under this voluntary program, cooperating foresters (participating private forestry consultants and industrial foresters) must comply with DNR standards and rules for all landowner assistance regarding land-management guidance and timber harvest. In 2004, the DNR Cooperating Forester Program listed 74 private consulting firms and 23 forest product companies (employing a total of 154 graduate foresters) that offer private forestry services.

INDUSTRIAL ASSISTANCE TO LANDOWNERS

As major wood-using companies recognized the need for a more reliable, long-term supply of wood, they developed industrial tree farm programs. Beginning in the mid-1960s, companies began offering services to landowners who wanted to manage and harvest their timber. These services vary between companies but usually include an inventory of the timber and preparation of a written forest-management plan, which includes owner's goals and technical advice for planning, planting, harvesting, and marketing timber crops. Some companies also provide site preparation, herbicide application, and planting services at an additional cost.

Often the company makes a "first right of refusal" agreement with the landowner, giving the company the first right to bid on any future timber sale on the land.

WISCONSIN WOODLAND OWNERS ASSOCIATION

The future of Wisconsin forestry depends not only on forests in state and county ownership but on the more than nine million acres in private ownership. The Wisconsin Woodland Owners Association Inc. (WWOA) grew out of a recommendation from the 1953 Wisconsin Silver Anniversary Forestry Conference in Milwaukee. At that conference, many people felt that there should be an organization of woodland owners interested in pursuing common goals and objectives associated with their forestland ownership. In 1976, the DNR Division of Forestry applied for a U.S. Forest Service grant and formed a partnership with UW–Madison to create Wisconsin's first woodland owners organization.

Woodland owners from across the state met on June 7, 1979, to formalize and create a shared vision for WWOA to advance the interests of woodland owners and the cause of forestry; to develop public appreciation for the value of Wisconsin woodlands

91

The Wisconsin Woodland Owners Association is a nonprofit educational organization established in 1979. Its objectives include encouraging the wise use of forests and their resources, fostering appreciation for woodlands, and educating those interested in managing the forest. Here WWOA past-president Marvin Meier addresses members at a field day in Lincoln County.

and their importance in the economy and overall welfare of the state; and to foster and encourage the wise use and management of the woodlands and all related resources in Wisconsin.

WWOA's strength is its members, who share their experiences with each other. Growing from 804 members in 1980, WWOA celebrates its 25th anniversary in 2004 with more than 2,300 members in 29 states and the United Kingdom. WWOA promotes good stewardship of Wisconsin woodlands by distributing educational materials, providing scholarships to organizations involved in environmental education or natural resource management, sponsoring traveling exhibits, holding workshops and field days, and informing legislators about woodland issues. WWOA has become a national leader among statewide woodland owner associations, and its members are leaders within Wisconsin's forestry community.

According to WWOA president Al Barden, "Clearly, WWOA speaks on behalf of the private timberland owner in Wisconsin. With a growing membership of over 2,300, the hundreds of landowners who attend WWOA's conferences, seminars, and field days annually, and those who serve WWOA in various leadership roles including

MORE HELP FOR WOODLAND OWNERS

A number of state and federal programs exist to help woodland owners who wish to manage their land on a sustainable basis. These programs encourage landowners to seek assistance and guidance from professional foresters through either the Wisconsin DNR or a private forestry consulting firm.

➤ The Wisconsin Forest Landowner Grant Program is a state cost-sharing program enacted in 1997 to make up for losses in federal support. It provides $1 million every year, with a maximum of $10,000 per landowner, for management-plan preparation, tree planting, timber stand improvement, soil and water protection, fencing, wildlife practices, fisheries practices, buffer establishments, species protection, and historic and aesthetic enhancements. Landowners must have a written management plan and own between 10 and 500 contiguous acres of nonindustrial forested land to participate.

➤ The Conservation Reserve Enhancement Program is a federal program that pays landowners to plant trees on sensitive lands. Cost sharing is available for wildlife plantings, grass establishment, erosion controls, and stream buffers.

➤ The Environmental Quality Incentives Program is a federal cost-sharing program (up to 75 percent) administered by the U.S. Department of Agriculture's Natural Resources Conservation Service (NRCS). Technical assistance is provided by the Wisconsin DNR and NRCS. The program offers landowners up to $10,000 annually for tree stock and planting, ecosystem management, erosion control on agricultural land, agricultural waste management, and stream buffers.

➤ The Wildlife Habitat Incentives Program is a federal cost-sharing program, capped at $10,000 per landowner, for wildlife plantings, grass establishment, fencing, prescribed burning, improvement of wildlife and fish habitat, wetland restoration, and farm buffer development.

providing information to legislators and state forestry staff, WWOA is and will continue to be a powerful voice of the private woodland owner in Wisconsin."

Partnering with the DNR, the University of Wisconsin–Extension, Wisconsin Forest Productivity Council, Wisconsin Tree Farm Committee, and other environmental and conservation organizations, WWOA has sponsored conferences, seminars, and workshops throughout Wisconsin to educate private woodland owners about all aspects of good forest stewardship.

WWOA's quarterly magazine, *Woodland Management*, shares the experiences of its members and provides advice on good forest management, the creation of wildlife habitat, and practices to prevent soil and water erosion. Other WWOA educational initiatives include field days, workshops, and management information on the local level for members of its 14 Wisconsin chapters. Its Web site, www.wisconsinwoodlands.org, is available for woodland owners to learn more about the association and sustainable forestry.

Private woodland owners can receive woodland-management assistance and information from many other groups, including the UW–Extension, USDA Natural Resources Conservation

Service, American Tree Farm System, Wisconsin Forest Productivity Council, Wisconsin Walnut Council, Wisconsin Maple Syrup Producers, Wisconsin Christmas Tree Growers, Forest Industry Safety and Training Alliance, Lake States Lumber Association, Community Forestry Resource Center, Ruffed Grouse Society, the Wisconsin chapter of the National Wild Turkey Federation, The Nature Conservancy, Wisconsin Family Forests, a number of forestry cooperatives, Wisconsin Forest Resources Education Alliance, Gathering Waters, and Wisconsin Geological and Natural History Survey.

A NEW FORESTRY LAW FOR LANDOWNERS

The Managed Forest Law of 1985 combined the provisions of the Forest Crop and Woodland Tax laws into one act that provided tax incentives to manage forest resources for multiple benefits. The key advantages of this law include a 25- or 50-year commitment to practice sustainable forestry; the deferral of property taxes; recognition of the landowner's objectives; the creation of a written management plan that ensures good forest stewardship; and the landowners' option to open or close some of their land to the public.

"The law is meant to maintain forestland and discourage people from breaking up parcels [of land]," stated Ken Hujanen, retired DNR forest tax law administrator. "The Managed Forest Law gets people thinking about sustainability and may lead to certification for some as they take it one step further."

Nearly 31,000 landowners have entered into this program. Today, more than 2.6 million acres of Wisconsin forestland are managed under all forest tax programs.

THE GOVERNOR'S COUNCIL ON FORESTRY

In 1981, Governor Lee Dreyfus created the Governor's Council on Forestry to advise the governor about policy issues related to forestry. The original council was established by executive order, but in 2002 the council was re-created by statute and plays an advocacy role on issues affecting Wisconsin's forests. The council consists of 19 people appointed by the governor, including the chief state forester, legislators, and representatives of academia, conservation, industry, and other public and private organizations. The council's quarterly meetings are open to the public.

THE GREAT LAKES FOREST ALLIANCE

Chartered in 1987 by the governors of the states of Wisconsin, Minnesota, and Michigan (the Canadian province of Ontario joined in 1997), the Great Lakes Forest Alliance's goal is to create an internationally recognized image of Great Lakes forest resources and their uses and values. Its trustees include chief and head foresters, academics, private woodland owners, conservation organizations, and tourism and timber representatives. Promoting long-term forestry objectives, economic health of the region, and conservation issues are among its many concerns.

A LASTING LEGACY

At the time of early European settlement, Wisconsin was a land of great forests. Then, its trees were brought down to make way for the plow, without an understanding of the nature of the land. The great success is that forestry, as practiced in Wisconsin, has reclaimed the Cutover and returned the state to beauty, biological diversity, and sustainable productivity.

With development and increasing forest fragmentation, tracts of forestland are being converted to nonforest uses. Addressing the need to protect land from future development, Congress passed the Forest Legacy Program as part of the 1990 Farm Bill. When implemented, Wisconsin's mission was "to minimize fragmentation and conversion of significant forested areas to non-forest uses, through the wise administration of conversion easements, that focus on the sustainable use of forest resources." To be accepted into the Forest Legacy Program, applicants must meet selected criteria, and preference is given to conservation groups or land trusts that can provide the monitoring needed to participate in the program.

During the past four decades, a multitude of new laws, organizations, ideas, and technologies has brought Wisconsin's forests to their present condition. Today, the state's forests contribute to clean air, clean water, abundant wildlife, and a foundation for economic stability, recreation, and quality of life.

CHAPTER SEVEN

WISCONSIN'S FORESTS TODAY
SUCCESSFUL EXAMPLES OF SUSTAINABLE FORESTRY

"THE FORESTS OF WISCONSIN, *like the legendary phoenix bird, have arisen from the smoke and ashes of a devastated pine empire to become once again a priceless natural resource."*

—Milton E. Reinke, Retired Chief State Forester, 1984

Of Wisconsin's 35 million acres of land, forest covers about 16 million acres or about 46 percent of the state's total land area. Forest inventories conducted periodically since 1936 by the U.S. Forest Service and the Wisconsin Conservation Department (now the Wisconsin Department of Natural Resources [DNR]), together with the first Assessment of Wisconsin Forests in 1985, provided important guidance to policymakers and to industry and forest users for long-term development, protection, and use of state forests. This information is critical to making wise forestry decisions.

Since 1968, the state's forest area has been steadily increasing, mostly from the conversion of marginal agricultural land back to forests. Between 1983 and 1996, the number of trees in the state taller than 10 feet increased by 1.4 billion. In 1996, Wisconsin had about 9.8 billion trees. There were 18.5 billion cubic feet of growing stock volume, of which 4.4 billion were conifer and 14.1 billion were hardwood. More than 95 percent of Wisconsin's standing forests are a result of natural regeneration. The remainder consists of plantations or areas reforested through planting and are sufficiently productive to qualify as timberland.

Wisconsin's forest resources can be divided

Covering almost half the state, Wisconsin forests are now healthier than at any time since the lumbering era.

WISCONSIN FOREST TYPES

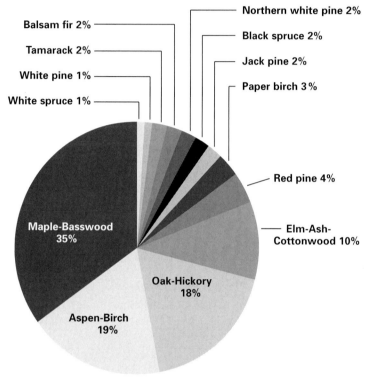

Balsam fir 2%
Tamarack 2%
White pine 1%
White spruce 1%
Northern white pine 2%
Black spruce 2%
Jack pine 2%
Paper birch 3%
Red pine 4%
Elm-Ash-Cottonwood 10%
Maple-Basswood 35%
Oak-Hickory 18%
Aspen-Birch 19%

The most abundant forest types in Wisconsin are hardwood forest types. Maple-basswood accounts for 5.3 million acres, followed by aspen-birch and oak-hickory. While 84 percent of Wisconsin's forests are hardwood types, there are also significant softwood types occupying large areas, especially in the north. Red pine, jack pine, black spruce, northern white cedar, white pine, and tamarack are the most common conifer forest types. Fifty-seven percent of Wisconsin's woodlands—more than nine million acres—are owned by private individuals and families.

into two broad categories: northern mixed forest and southern broadleaf forest. This divide exists in Wisconsin because of differences in the effects of glaciation, soil types, and climates of the northern and southern parts of the state. These two regions meet in an area called the "tension zone," which stretches across Wisconsin from northwest to southeast in an S shape. This zone contains representative plant and animal species from both the northern mixed forest and the southern broadleaf forest.

THE PROFESSION OF FORESTRY TODAY

Professional foresters carry the responsibilities of managing forests and further advancing the practice of sustainable forestry. Today's foresters follow in the footsteps of the first state forester hired in 1904 as scientists who manage forest resources.

In addition to timber management and fire-control duties, today's foresters are concerned with water quality, wildlife, endangered resources, and recreational opportunities associated with forests. "Forestry is not just about growing trees, but also protecting watersheds so we have good water, providing habitat for wildlife, and providing opportunities for outdoor recreation, among

other things," according to Miles Benson, former chairman of the Wisconsin chapter of the Society of American Foresters.[1]

FOREST REGENERATION THROUGH HARVESTING

Foresters have many tools to improve woodlands, including harvesting. Foresters choose a harvest system based on the species they want to regenerate or perpetuate; stand characteristics such as soil type, topography, and aspect; and the landowner's objectives. Woodland owners have many reasons for owning their land. It may be to produce timber, create wildlife habitat, protect a watershed, enjoy its aesthetic value, or use it for recreation. Achieving these goals can require some form of forest management, possibly timber harvesting. There are several options when timber harvesting is called for, including the following.

Clear-Cutting. This removes all trees from part of a mature stand. A new stand grows from root or stump sprouts, from seeds of surrounding trees, from seeds spread manually over the harvest area, or from planting seedlings. Clear-cutting favors trees that do not tolerate shade well, such as aspen, cottonwood, jack pine, red pine, paper birch, and black cherry.

Seed Tree. The seed tree system is similar to clear-cutting except that certain mature trees, called seed trees, are left standing to furnish seed for natural restocking. After the new forest becomes established, the seed trees are usually removed. The seed tree method has one advantage over clear-cutting—it is not necessary to wait for a good seed year before the main harvest.

Shelterwood. The shelterwood harvest involves two or three harvest operations, through which some trees are left to grow, cast seed, and provide shelter for the new stand. The shelter trees are harvested after seedlings become established. The shelterwood system normally requires a minimum of two cuttings. Frequently, foresters use this system to regenerate yellow birch, basswood, and white pine.

Single-Tree Selection. The single-tree selection system relies on frequent cuts and encourages shade-tolerant species. It creates and maintains uneven-aged stands by removing mature timber either as single, scattered trees or in small groups. During each cut, foresters remove undesirable trees, thin overly dense areas, and harvest mature trees. Stands with mature trees are commonly harvested at approximately 10- to 15-year intervals to minimize harvest costs and

Wisconsin is considered the leader among states in forest-product manufacturing. Billions of dollars of economic impact are generated each year from our state's forests.

residual stand damage. The selection system best nurtures the shade-tolerant seedlings of the sugar maple–dominated northern hardwood forest.

NURSERIES AND SEEDLINGS

Another tool used by foresters is reforestation with seedlings. Wisconsin's state forest nursery program and private tree nurseries together produce millions of seedlings each year for reforestation and conservation purposes. These small seedlings make a big difference in the environment, enhancing wildlife habitat, restoring rare ecosystems, conserving energy, reducing soil erosion, improving water quality, increasing aesthetic beauty, and providing raw materials necessary for a strong forest products industry.

During the 2003 spring season, state nurseries distributed about 15.6 million native tree and shrub seedlings. Private and industrial nurseries produced about 4 million additional tree seedlings in 2003. This combined effort accounted for about 25,000 acres reforested in Wisconsin.

The DNR operates three state nurseries, which combined produce 18–20 million seedlings annually. Private-sector nurseries provide several million additional seedlings annually for reforestation. Pictured here is the Wilson Nursery near Boscobel.

FIRE AS A MANAGEMENT TOOL

With increased knowledge about forest

ecology, ideas about fire have changed. Gradually, it has become clear that fire is a part of nature and cannot be completely excluded from the forest. It is and always has been part of the forest ecosystem. Fire can maintain existing forest conditions, retard or promote successional patterns, release or recycle essential nutrients, regenerate a dying forest, improve habitat for wildlife, and modify the impact of insects and disease.

Fire is used as a tool for forest management under the concept of prescribed burning. A prescribed burn is a controlled fire under known weather and fuel conditions to attain a predictable management objective. Wildlife managers use it, for example, to create improved habitat or to maintain waterfowl or sharp-tailed grouse areas. Foresters sometimes use it to prepare seedbeds and planting sites after logging. They also use it to prevent wildfires by reducing the amount of slash left after logging operations and to lessen the risk of serious fires during dry periods. It is also used to maintain some rare ecosystems such as prairie and savanna.

GLOBAL PERSPECTIVE

Concern about worldwide forest destruction has created a demand for products that are made from well-managed forests. Wisconsin's forests are

a small but important part of the global ecosystem.

Forest certification is a voluntary marketplace approach to encourage responsible forestry. Products from certified forests are tracked from stump to final product, and those products are labeled so customers know they came from a well-managed forest.

Several certification programs are available to landowners. Performance-based programs require landowners to meet standards that are independently set and use specific measures to monitor on-the-ground performance. Other programs are systems-based, relying on general standards that conform to sustainable forestry principles. Yet others are a combination of the two. Among the certification programs available are American Tree Farm System, Forest Stewardship Council (FSC), ISO 14001, Sustainable Forestry Initiative (SFI), and the Green Tag program. Wisconsin's designated state forests received FSC and SFI certification in 2004.[2]

WISCONSIN'S FORESTS TODAY

Wisconsin's forests are growing faster than they are being cut, with loggers removing approximately 70 percent of the net annual growth. However, the global demand for wood products,

Forest certification is a voluntary approach to encourage responsible forestry. Some products from certified forests are tracked from harvest to final product. Those products are labeled so customers know that they came from a well-managed forest. Currently, less than 1 percent of the world's annual harvest comes from certified forests. Price premiums for "green" wood products are currently small or nonexistent. Both of these conditions are expected to increase.

THE EVOLUTION OF FIRE-FIGHTING EQUIPMENT

Fire-fighting equipment has changed considerably over the past century. In the early twentieth century, fire wardens and firefighters provided their own equipment, which usually consisted of a shovel or an ax and sometimes gunnysacks or burlap bags. By 1911, patrolmen were furnished with canvas buckets to use where water was available. Backpack pumps came into general use in about 1918. In those days, backfiring and building fire lines with horse-drawn plows represented state-of-the-art fire-fighting techniques.

Firefighters traveled, for the most part, on foot or horseback because roads were few and often impassable for vehicles. Sometimes logging railroads offered the best or only access to isolated areas. Here "pedes," or hand-operated railroad velocipedes, were widely used. In 1914, the state noted with pride that it owned 1 motor-powered and 10 hand-operated railroad speeders. With the development of roads, horse-drawn vehicles came into use. The state purchased its first motor truck for hauling firefighters and supplies in 1915. In 1917, the use of auto patrols began, and they soon came into general use.

In 1915, Wisconsin became the first state to use an airplane for forest-fire detection. The plane, a Curtis Flying Boat, had the ability to land on and take off from water. Lack of communication with the ground and difficulty flying in windy weather, however, limited its effectiveness.

CCC workers leave for a fire in 1937. Early fire-fighting equipment shown here includes a hose trailer, Caterpillar tractor, and fire plow.

By 1927, headquarters buildings and a truck with a power pump, water tank, hose, and hand tools for fighting fires had been provided for each of the established fire-protection districts. A system of 54 lookout towers and 400 miles of telephone line provided direct contact among patrolmen. The plow came into its own as standard fire-fighting equipment with the use of the Caterpillar tractor in about 1930.

During the 1930s, L. W. Lembcke invented fire-fighting equipment that is the basis for the modern equipment used today. Examples include a fire-line plow with coulter, a tilting platform

A DNR firefighter works to extinguish a fire as it approaches a fire break.

Federal Communications Commission approved the use of ultra-high-frequency radios in early 1938. The Conservation Department immediately equipped primary fire tower crews, rangers' vehicles, and planes with radios.

Today much of the work of fire fighting is done by the tractor-plow and wildfire engines. Each of the state's 56 fire-response units has a forest ranger equipped with a modern initial-attack 4x4 wildfire engine, an engine able to hold 850 gallons of water with pumps, and a tractor-plow unit.

Aircraft are used along with fire towers to detect fires, and specially equipped aircraft known as single-engine air tankers drop retardant from the air to help control forest fires. Planes also serve a critical safety role by observing firefighters in hazardous situations and providing intelligence about a forest fire. While early lookout towers served only to observe fire, modern towers have two-way radios to facilitate communication with dispatchers and initial attack crews. During the 1997 fire season, the DNR staffed 97 fire towers in Wisconsin in addition to other means of fire detection, including citizen reporting and aerial sighting.

Today the DNR uses automated weather stations, which collect moisture and temperature data and electronically transmit the data to a central computer to predict fire danger. Wisconsin has a network of 26 weather stations, which closely monitor forest-fire conditions across the state.

trailer to transport plows and tractors, a heavy-duty pumper-trailer to transport water to a fire, and a standard trailer hitch for department cars and trucks. The "Wisconsin Plow" was the forerunner of the plows now used in many other parts of the country for fire fighting. These and numerous other devices initiated the modern era of mechanical forest-fire control.

Also during this decade, the Wisconsin Conservation Department began using airplanes on a regular basis for fire detection and for reconnaissance during fires. After some futile attempts to use radios in fire prevention and fire fighting, the

103

including those from Wisconsin forests, is increasing annually. Paper, timber, furniture, crates—even syrup and wild mushrooms—are in increasing demand. The forests of Wisconsin are some of the best managed in the world. Thus, importing wood from elsewhere to satisfy our needs might well perpetuate the type of poor management in other countries that Wisconsin experienced at the turn of the twentieth century. The stability of Wisconsin's forest industry provides stability for the Wisconsin economy.

Private landowners collectively own about 10 million acres, nearly two-thirds of the state's total of almost 16 million wooded acres. The roughly 260,000 individuals, families, and nontimber companies that own the land are motivated by many objectives. In the past, woods owned by farmers were considered to be less important than cropland was. But that has changed radically in the last 50 years. Private forests have become some of the most highly valued property in Wisconsin. There is no doubt today about the impact private forests have on clean water and air, improved wildlife habitat, places to hunt and hike, and a thriving economy. In terms of value-added commercial products alone, raw materials from these private lands are manufactured into goods

worth an estimated $12.8 billion annually.

County forests make up the largest percentage of Wisconsin's public forests. They cover 2.3 million acres in 29 counties. In 2002, county forests produced 11.8 million board feet of saw logs and 614,645 cords worth more than $18 million. This timber helps to sustain more than 30,000 full-time jobs in logging, trucking, paper production, and manufactured building materials. In 2001 and 2002, almost 4.2 million trees were planted in county forests.

In addition to the timber resources, county forests are available to the general public for a variety of recreational activities. Within these two million-plus acres are more than 1,200 campsites and thousands of miles of hiking, skiing, and snowmobile trails, as well as public access to hundreds of lakes and streams.

State forests cover nearly one-half million acres. Timber sales in 2002 totaled $3.3 million, with almost half of that value coming from timber harvested from the Northern Highland–American Legion State Forest. As with county forests, recreation is a primary use of Wisconsin's state forests. Nearly three million people enjoyed the recreational opportunities of Wisconsin's state forests in 2000. The Northern Highland–American

Legion State Forest welcomed nearly two million of those visitors. Almost half of the people who visit state forests enjoy day-use recreation such as boating, fishing, or hunting. Other popular activities include camping, swimming, picnicking, snowmobiling, and all-terrain-vehicle riding.

While the purpose of state forests has arguably remained fundamentally the same since their beginnings, the priority of public benefits derived from them has evolved, placing greater emphasis on nontimber values, including recreational uses. For example, after the federal government recognized the St. Croix River as a National Scenic Riverway in 1968, Wisconsin established the St. Croix River State Forest (now known as Governor Knowles State Forest) in 1970 to provide a buffer for the federally designated area. While the plan for the state forest provided for forest management, including timber harvest and tree planting, protection and preservation of the unique character of the river itself was now the major goal. Aesthetics, solitude, and biodiversity are increasingly important considerations in management of state forests.

Wisconsin is home to one national forest, the Chequamegon–Nicolet National Forest, which accounts for 9 percent of the state's forestland. In 1996, the Chequamegon–Nicolet contained 968 million trees, approximately 10 percent of all trees found in Wisconsin.

Forest management is important in the Chequamegon–Nicolet National Forest. Timber harvesting is managed to provide wildlife habitat, improve forest health, increase productivity, maintain ecosystems, and supply forest products. From 1986 through 1995, the Chequamegon–Nicolet provided nearly 1.4 billion board feet of sawtimber and pulpwood worth $37.5 million. Yet growth actually exceeded removals by more than 10 percent during this period. Hundreds of people annually purchase permits to gather fir boughs, ornamental greens, Christmas trees, firewood, and cones.

The value of the Chequamegon–Nicolet National Forest to the state and local economies is not measured solely by the sale of forest products, however. Improving forest health, maintaining forest ecosystems, and providing a variety of wildlife habitats and recreational opportunities are key benefits. National forest staff work jointly with the other public land managers to provide for the full range of forest communities and species important to Wisconsin. Hunters, hikers, nature lovers, and the tourism industry all reap the benefits of sustainable forest management. Forty-seven

developed campgrounds, and almost-unlimited sites for primitive camping are available. The forest has more than 1,400 miles of trails for hiking, mountain biking, horseback riding, snowmobiling, cross-country skiing, and riding all-terrain vehicles. Auto routes include the Lakewood Auto Tour, the Heritage Scenic Byway, and the Great Divide Scenic Tour.

FORESTS AS OUTDOOR CLASSROOMS

The future of the state's forests depends on public knowledge and awareness of the role of sustainable forest management in society. Forests serve as a classroom for students, and there is no better teaching tool than hands-on experience.

Wisconsin has more than 400 registered school or community forests, covering more than 67,000 acres. School forests were originally intended to demonstrate timber management and help replant trees. Today they are increasingly used for environmental education. Forty-two percent have demonstration areas, and 11 percent have classrooms or lecture halls. Seventy-one percent have nature trails, and 55 percent have hiking trails.

Created in 1927, then revised in 1947 and again in 1985, what is now known as the

Each year millions of dollars worth of timber are logged, and thousands of people enjoy camping, hiking, biking, and fishing in Wisconsin's forests. Our forests are home to thousands of plant and animal species.

The school forest program in the United States began in Wisconsin. School forests keep communities connected with the natural world and provide income and ecological benefits for the community.

Community Forests Law allows cities, villages, and school districts to own land, engage in forestry, receive free planting stock from state forest nurseries, and use the services of foresters in preparing and carrying out planting and forest-management plans.

Prior to 1990, any size parcel could be registered as a school forest. Current requirements are that registered parcels must be dedicated to forestry, have a minimum of 1 acre, a width of at least 120 feet, and be at least 80 percent forested. In 1990, a new state mandate required Wisconsin school districts to integrate environmental education into kindergarten through grade 12 (K-12) curriculum plans. As Gene Francisco, former chief state forester, remarked in 2001, "Our school forests are valuable outdoor classrooms for all ages and can be used in all subject areas. In an increasingly urban society, school forests help us make the connection between the value of healthy forests and our social, economic, and ecological needs. On a more direct level, school forests connect forest resources to a student's everyday needs."

To facilitate the use of school forests as outdoor classrooms, the DNR Division of Forestry and the Wisconsin Center for Environmental

Education at UW–Stevens Point cooperatively established the Learning, Activities & Experiences in Forestry (LEAF) program in 2001. LEAF promotes the development, dissemination, implementation, and evaluation of forestry education programs in Wisconsin schools. Beginning in 2004, it has trained teachers, provided a K-12 forestry activity guide, offered partnerships with other Wisconsin K-12 forestry education stakeholders, and assisted schools in developing their school forest plans.

To provide additional emphasis for students in southeastern Wisconsin, the Wisconsin Woodland Owners Association (WWOA) Foundation opened the 131-acre Seno Woodland Management Center, dedicated to forestry education and research, in Walworth and Kenosha Counties in 1994. Hundreds of students visit each year to learn about forestry. In addition, the Wisconsin DNR is developing a Forestry Education Center in Milwaukee County to provide hands-on learning about all aspects of sustainable forestry.

THE ECONOMICS OF WISCONSIN FORESTS

In 1996, the state produced timber worth roughly $210 million, most of it—72 percent— logged from privately owned forestlands, followed by federal, county, and state-owned lands.

Most of the timber stumpage value in 1996 came from the central and southwestern parts of the state and included high-value species such as walnut and oak. While the forests of the northern part of the state produced the highest volumes, much of the harvest consisted of lower-value species such as aspen and birch.

The economic benefits of Wisconsin's forests reach beyond the dollar value of logged lumber. More than 1,800 Wisconsin timber companies employ over 100,000 people in the state, with a total payroll of more than $4.5 billion. In 2000, timber production provided a partial basis for primary, secondary, and reconstituted wood production that accounted for approximately 6 percent of Wisconsin's gross state product (roughly $20 billion of $330 billion). Value-added wood industries and reconstituted wood products are important economic contributors to the state's economy. The reconstituted wood products, primarily pulp and paper, dominate with more than $14 billion of output and more than 50,000 jobs, which pay salaries 60 percent higher than the state average. While the pulp and paper industry employs only 1.5 percent of the state's workforce, the wages it pays account for 3 percent

SENO WOODLAND MANAGEMENT CENTER

Dr. Elvira Seno willed that her 131 acres be dedicated to forest education and research. The Seno property's greatest strength is the opportunity to show visitors sound land use, practical research, and forest management on a smaller scale.

As a child, Elvira Seno lived with her family near Burlington, and she enjoyed visiting friends who lived on a 131-acre farm to the east. When Dr. Seno retired in 1974, she bought the land she had visited as a child. During the 20 years she lived there, she planted almost 50,000 trees, removed brushy invaders, culled weak saplings, and harvested mature trees. She realized that the only way to make sure the property stayed the way she wanted was to find someone who could guarantee it would not be developed. She tried to interest several organizations and finally turned to other woodland owners through a nonprofit educational foundation of WWOA. Seno stipulated that the property be used for active research on issues faced by private landowners. One of her goals was to provide a forest learning center for area schools, forest landowners, and the area's large urban population. The center's location, easily accessible from Milwaukee, Madison, Chicago, Janesville, and Beloit, is ideal to meet this goal. The center, five miles south of Burlington, is slowly taking shape. Plans call for creating research plots to demonstrate erosion-control techniques; creating techniques to plant and harvest trees to maintain water quality; providing urban residents with opportunities to study trees; and creating programs for woodland owners.

107

of all wages paid to Wisconsin workers.

According to the Department of Urban and Regional Planning at UW–Madison, papermaking indirectly supports jobs for 152,000 people in the state. This translates to almost $4.5 billion of economic benefit to the state from wages spent for goods and services from these support industries and service businesses. Wisconsin's forests provide the raw materials not only for lumber and paper but also for medicines, paints, plastics, and many other products. Production by Wisconsin wood-using companies is valued at over $20 billion annually. Private lands supply more than 72 percent of the raw materials. In 28 counties, the forest-products industry is the largest employer; in another 14, it is ranked in the top three. Wisconsin is first in the nation in paper production and in forest industry value of shipments and is second in employee compensation.

SOCIAL AND CULTURAL VALUES OF FORESTS

Some of the most deeply felt and complex values related to forests are in the social and cultural arenas. Whether for aesthetic enjoyment, a legacy to be passed to future generations, a part of one's cultural heritage, or a place to renew one's spirit,

Wisconsin's forests are valued for cultural and social reasons. This is particularly evident in a survey conducted in 1998 by the DNR, in which Wisconsin residents ranked the importance of conservation of natural resources and recreation a 9 on a scale of 1 to 10.

Among the most important aspects of social value are the recreational benefits that Wisconsin's forests offer. Each year, millions of people enjoy hunting, camping, snowmobiling, hiking, fishing, all-terrain-vehicle use, wildlife watching, biking, and more in Wisconsin's forests. And a number of activities, such as a walking, jogging, and pleasure driving, are enhanced by forests.

Within Wisconsin's forests are many cultural resources, including historic structures, archaeological sites, cemeteries, and traditional-use areas. While these sites may not provide the economic opportunities other forest uses do, they are equally as important. Cultural resource conservation often contributes to soil, water, and wildlife habitat conservation measures. It may affect resale value of the land, as the resource may be used for developing a sense of corporate or community identity that encourages new investment. Some federal and state laws provide financial incentives to preserve and protect cultural resources.

ECOLOGICAL VALUES OF FORESTS

Historically, fire was an important natural disturbance factor in Wisconsin's forests, both northern and southern. However, in the last 50 years, fire has been largely eliminated from the forest. Protecting human lives and property from the effects of fire has resulted in many significant changes to forest ecosystem composition, structure, and function. While fire protection remains very important to people owning or living near forests, there is increasing awareness of the ecological importance of fire, and more prescribed burns are occurring in restoration areas. Some ecosystems, such as oak savannas, barrens, and prairies, require fire to regenerate and maintain their species composition.

Wisconsin has over 30,000 miles of rivers and streams and more than 15,000 lakes. The glaciation of northern Wisconsin created the rich legacy of water bodies and wetlands in our present landscape. In general, forests help maintain water quality by holding soil and preventing erosion. Most of the high-quality streams and lakes in the state are located in forests. However, there is the potential for nonpoint-source pollution from forestry practices affecting the state's water resources.

FORESTS FOR RECREATION

More than 200,000 registered snowmobilers hit Wisconsin's 25,000 miles of groomed trails each winter. The forests generate millions of dollars of revenue when people visit them to hike, bike, fish, camp, and snowmobile.

In the first half of the nineteenth century, vast hunting preserves and expensive private lodges dotted northern Wisconsin. In 1897, hunters and anglers spent $20,000 annually in the region. Early on, E. M. Griffith recognized the full potential for recreation in northern Wisconsin. In 1912, Griffith estimated the area could generate $677,444 (approximately $13 million in 2004 dollars) annually from tourism. He predicted, "The forest reserve region should become in time a great summer resort for people throughout the entire Mississippi Valley." Indeed, Griffith expected the region to rival the Adirondacks of the East as a resort area.

In the early twentieth century, wealthy vacationers came by train to elegant resort hotels and picturesque private lodges. With the introduction of automobiles in the early 1900s, and a subsequent expanding network of improved roads, private recreational lakeshore development expanded. Lakeside cottages and cabins became economically feasible for the upper middle class. The automobile completely altered the concept of how forests should be used. Automobile-led recreation was a crucial factor in the emerging debate between forest usage and preservation. During this time, most Cutover counties made plans for lakefront swimming beaches, fishing sites, and hiking trails and expanded the nonagricultural uses of northern Wisconsin land. Recognition of the particular attraction of water-based recreation prompted a movement to acquire more general public access to lakes and streams. As early as the 1930s, the tourism industry provided substantial, although seasonal, employment.

After World War II, personal incomes, the amount of leisure time, and automobile ownership rose dramatically. The summer vacation became a middle-class necessity, and the automobile allowed urban families to vacation in northern Wisconsin. As a result, the forests became an integral part of the region's new economy and drew millions of tourists each year.

Today, Wisconsin forests provide a vast array of recreational opportunities, which contribute dollars to the state's economy. Wisconsin households spend more than $5.5 billion per year on goods and services associated with forest-based recreation. In addition, many nonresidents visit Wisconsin expressly for forest-based recreation. The dollars they spend provide additional income for local businesses.

109

Garlic mustard is an invasive species that disrupts the sensitive ecosystem. Campers, hikers, and others are asked to assist efforts in reducing the spread of garlic mustard by pulling the plant when they find it.

Nonpoint-source pollution, which accounts for about half of all pollutants entering our nation's waters, occurs when water from rainfall or snowmelt moves across the ground, transporting pollutants into streams, lakes, wetlands, or groundwater. In Wisconsin, it is estimated that only 3 percent of nonpoint pollution comes from forestry practices. Wisconsin's forestry BMPs for Water Quality are voluntary guidelines to help loggers, landowners, and natural resource managers minimize nonpoint-source pollution during forestry operations. The use of BMPs is a practical and cost-effective way to ensure that forestry activities do not harm water quality.

A key component of sustainability in today's forests is biodiversity. John Curtis described about 40 distinct Wisconsin terrestrial communities in the 1950s. Most of these are still intact. However, savannas and barrens have experienced striking decline. Forests that have never been disturbed are also uncommon. In 1995, L. E. Frelich, a University of Minnesota professor, estimated that 58,500 acres—less than 0.4 percent—of Wisconsin's forests had not experienced severe human disturbance since European settlement. Seventy-nine percent of this area is white cedar forests; another 10 percent is black spruce–tamarack forest.

GYPSY MOTH DESTRUCTION

Gypsy moths are now found throughout Wisconsin. The hairy caterpillar can be identified by its five pairs of blue spots followed by six pairs of red spots along the back.

Since the 1990s, Wisconsin has been battling gypsy moths, destructive defoliators of shade, fruit, and forest trees across the eastern United States. Professor L. Trouvelotin brought the insects to North America more than a century ago in a misguided attempt to breed a hardy silkworm. Their migration from the northeast and mid-Atlantic states occurred with the help of wind and inadvertent transport by people on recreational vehicles, cars, nursery stock, firewood, and outdoor furniture.

Gypsy moths defoliate primarily hardwood trees, although they do feed on some conifers. In pure conifer stands, defoliation is usually minimal. The effects of gypsy-moth defoliation can make trees more susceptible to attack by other pests, such as the two-lined chestnut borer and shoestring root rot. Healthy trees can often tolerate or resist secondary attacks, while trees in poor health have a higher risk of death.

As of 2003, the gypsy moth had been found in all Wisconsin counties. Once established, the moth goes through a cycle of low population for about 10 years, followed by a population explosion (called an outbreak) that causes heavy defoliation, typically lasting one to two years.

In 2000, the DNR developed a Gypsy Moth Suppression Program to attempt to reduce outbreak populations using aerially applied insecticide. Besides using insecticides, timber harvesting and intermediate thinnings can be used to reduce food quality and shelter for the moth larvae and pupae. Intermediate thinnings, such as crop tree release, improve crown condition and vigor of the remaining trees, increasing their ability to survive defoliation. Other practices to help combat gypsy moth effects include removing gypsy moth—preferred tree species that are small and poor in quality; eliminating trees with large numbers of dead branches and rough and peeling bark that could create habitat for moths; and increasing nonpreferred species such as maple, hickory, black cherry, and ash in oak stands.

111

There are estimated to be about 2,300 species of vascular plants in the state of Wisconsin. About 1,800 of these are native to the state; 22 percent are believed to be introduced exotics. More than 650 species of vertebrates live in the state. In addition to fairly conspicuous species, there are also thousands of species of nonvascular plants and invertebrates, as well as fungi, bacteria, and protozoa—most of which have not yet been adequately described or researched. Human activities since Euramerican settlement have dramatically altered the distribution and abundance of many species. As of 1998, 241 species were listed on the state's endangered or threatened list, and 15 Wisconsin species are on the federal endangered or threatened list (11 species appear on both lists). Of the plant species listed, 28 percent are forest species, all of the listed mammals are forest species, 50 percent of listed bird species are forest species, and 40 percent of listed reptiles and amphibians are forest species.

Wisconsin's forests have been assailed by a variety of introduced exotic species. Exotic species can overwhelm the ecological capability of an area because they have not developed in conjunction with the natural ecosystem, and frequently there are no checks on their populations.

Exotic species can sometimes outcompete and crowd out native species. As nonnative species invade natural ecosystems and crowd out native species, they disrupt the ecosystem by reducing biodiversity. Dutch elm disease, chestnut blight, the European gypsy moth, and the Asian long-horned beetle are some of the major exotic threats to Wisconsin's forests. In addition, plants such as garlic mustard, buckthorn, and multiflora rose can take over a forest understory, effectively eliminating native plants from the area.

The DNR monitors the presence and spread of invasive species and pests and works to remove exotics and repopulate with native species.

LAND FRAGMENTATION

As rural Wisconsin becomes more densely populated, the average parcel size of privately owned forestland is getting smaller. Fragmentation of parcels is caused in part by land passing from one generation to another. Increasing land values and taxes make subdivision and sale of land attractive. Buyers seek forestland for home sites, recreation, aesthetics, and to have "their corner of the earth."

Implications of changing ownership are significant. Timber growing on small tracts that are also home sites often is excluded from harvest

for wood products. Residential development requires additional public services that cost communities more than they receive from increased tax revenues. Continued population growth, fragmentation of forestland, and construction of homes in forested areas increases the threat of forest fires. Fragmentation and the resulting development frequently change the forest cover and composition, creating conditions that no longer meet the needs of indigent species.

A LOOK AT SEVERAL WISCONSIN FORESTS

Following are brief descriptions of four examples of the many different types of forests in Wisconsin today.

Cathedral Pines. When Holt Lumber Company logged the area around Archibald, southwest of Lakewood in Oconto County, it decided to leave a stand of white and red pine uncut. Today only a few scattered stands, like Cathedral Pines, provide direct evidence of the character of the pre-European settlement.

Cathedral Pines contains white pines more than 300 years old. Like the white pine stands of the past, most trees are 20 to 30 inches in diameter, but some are three to four feet in diameter and well over 100 feet tall. The large crowns of the mature trees found in Cathedral Pines reach upward to form a nearly continuous canopy. The floor of the forest is open and relatively easy to walk through, except where an occasional large tree has fallen and created an opening in the canopy. The shrub and herbaceous layer is generally inconspicuous.

Adjacent to Cathedral Pines is a stand of old-growth hemlock. This old-growth forest also contains beech, sugar maple, yellow birch, and red and white pines. The understory is a mixture of witch hazel, baneberry, beech drops, blue-bead lily, maidenhair, and wood ferns. The Nature Conservancy purchased the land from the Holt and DeWitt families in 1991 and transferred it to the U.S. Forest Service in April 1993, and it now is part of the Chequamegon–Nicolet National Forest.

The Moquah Barrens. Pine barrens originally covered about 2.3 million acres in Wisconsin. The largest area occupied a long, narrow, glacial outwash plain with extremely coarse and nutrient-poor, sandy soils that stretched from Polk County to Bayfield County in the northwestern part of the state. The excessive drainage made the region prone to drought and frequent forest fires and produced vegetation dominated by grasses, forbs, shrubs, and scattered stands of trees. The most common tree

Development in Wisconsin's woodlands can lead to fragmentation, as parcels are broken into smaller sizes because of increased land values. Fragmentation can result in habitat loss, as the changes to the forest prevent it from regenerating as it typically would. In addition, development within the forest increases the threat of forest fires.

113

Cathedral Pines is a 20-acre parcel of 200- to 400-year-old pines located within the Chequamegon–Nicolet National Forest. It is located three miles south of Lakewood in Oconto County.

114

was usually jack pine. Important shrubs included sweet fern, red root, huckleberry, and blueberry. As a result of better fire protection beginning in the 1920s, dense pine forest began to replace the pine barrens and resulted in a great reduction in open land.

In 1938, wildlife biologists conducted a study of sharp-tailed grouse in the section of the pine barrens near Iron River known as the Moquah Barrens. Their report recommended the preservation of forest openings for sharp-tailed management. sharp-tailed grouse thrive only where they have a suitable combination of openings and brush or young forest. In 1950, the Wisconsin Conservation Department and the U.S. Forest Service cooperatively began an active management program to benefit sharp-tailed grouse in the Chequamegon National Forest. They selected for management an area of some 3,000 acres located eight miles northeast of Iron River.

The management plan focused on maintaining existing openings and creating new connecting openings. Previously, such conventional land-clearing techniques as bulldozing, herbicide spraying, and hand clearing had been used. These methods, however, proved slow, laborious, and expensive. As a result, the Wisconsin Conservation

Department and the U.S. Forest Service decided to use controlled fire as an efficient, inexpensive tool to clear 170 acres on the Moquah Barrens. It was the first major controlled burn for wildlife on national forestland in Wisconsin. Currently, the Moquah Wildlife Area totals 8,000 acres, and the U.S. Forest Service has targeted 2,800 surrounding acres for restoration.

The Menominee Forest. Wisconsin's forests are significantly different from those that existed before European settlement. Few remnants still exist of the forest that the early explorers saw and so vividly described. Today the Menominee Indian Reservation contains the largest block of old white pine–hardwood forest remaining in the Lake States, as well as several large, uncut cedar swamps.

Forest covers 93 percent of the land in Menominee County, while surrounding counties have only about 50 percent forest coverage. The Menominee forest "presents a remarkable reminder of how the Great Lakes Forest looked before the epic logging," according to author Duncan Harkin.[3] This is largely because the Menominee forest was not subjected to the unsustainable level of cutting that occurred in other parts of northern Wisconsin. Instead, sustainable forestry has been practiced on this forest since the early twentieth century.

The forests in Menominee County carry three times the board-foot volume per acre of the average Wisconsin woodland. Menominee County, the reservation of the Menomonee Indians since 1854, with its dense stands of tall white pines, presents a remarkable reminder of how parts of northern Wisconsin looked before the lumbering era.

115

Many landowners practice sustainable forestry. The American Tree Farm System is one program that helps small landowners, like Don and Rachel Jordan of Dodgeville, do so. The program requires that you own more than 10 acres of forestland, have a management plan, actively manage the forest, protect it from fire and insects, protect water quality, and provide for wildlife and recreation.

When the federal government established the Menominee Indian Reservation in 1854, the land contained an estimated 1.5 billion board feet of lumber. Between 1865 and 1988, more than 2.5 billion board feet of lumber was cut. Yet the most recent inventory estimates that the Menominee forest still contains at least 1.7 billion board feet of lumber. The backbone of the Menominee forestry program is its continuous inventory system, which measures changes in the forest to help determine the long-term effects of forest management. Knowing the inventory data allows foresters to consider options available to maximize stand volume and quality. As Marshall Pecore, Menominee Tribal Enterprises forest manager, wrote in 1992, "The Menominee people have balanced the concept of long-term, sustained-yield forest management with the shorter-term, diverse considerations of community stability and economic development."[4]

Jordan Tree Farm. Private woodlands are the future of Wisconsin's forests. As budgets, public pressure, and politics limit the management of public lands for wood products, private, nonindustrial forests offer the best alternative to satisfy the increasing demand for forest products. Wisconsin is a leader in voluntary and incentive programs to assist, encourage, and educate private woodland owners who wish to manage their forests sustainably.

The 773-acre tree farm of Don and Rachel Jordan of Dodgeville is a model for other private landowners. Rachel's parents originally purchased the land in 1947. The Jordans took ownership of the farm in 1981 and formed a limited partnership with their children to manage the land and its resources. The Jordans, active members of the Wisconsin Woodland Owners Association, worked with professional foresters to develop a written management plan. Their goals included growing high-quality hardwood timber, improving the forest stands, improving wildlife habitat, maintaining trails, and growing wildflowers. Based on their goals, a forester reviews the plan every five years with the Jordans and periodically inspects the stands to ensure that the actions on the land continue to meet the management plan.

The Jordans have been active in WWOA and the Wisconsin forest community to educate others on the benefits of sustainable forestry. Rachel Jordan is past-president of WWOA and a former member of the Governor's Council on Forestry.

In 1996, the American Tree Farm System honored the Jordans as the National Tree Farmers of the Year, the first winners from Wisconsin. Their success inspires other nonindustrial private woodland owners to sustainably manage their lands with a stewardship ethic.

PERPETUAL CHANGE

A century ago, E. M. Griffith was hired to restore Wisconsin's once dense, expansive forests. While change did not come quickly, and often the process was difficult and challenging, 100 years later, Wisconsin forests are healthier than at any time since the turn of the century. Residents enjoy a higher quality of life because of the forests and the cultural, ecological, economic, and social benefits they provide.

Wisconsin's forests will continue to change as a result of forest growth, natural succession, human disturbance, fire, weather, insects, disease, and the effects of wildlife. Such changes have occurred for thousands of years and will continue into the future. In addition, the forest will come under increasing demand to fulfill a variety of human needs. Forestry in the future will have to develop new strategies to meet growing and sometimes conflicting uses, but Wisconsin's healthy forests of today provide testimony to progress made since the turn of the century. An interested and enlightened public along with dedicated professionals and involved private landowners will surely prevail.

"For me, the word that best sums up a common sense approach to ecology is 'balance.' Balance of human and non-human interests, balance of environment and economy, balance of reason and emotion. We cannot deny that we must consume to survive any more than we can deny that over-consumption would lead to our demise. A world without beauty is as unthinkable as a world without food, and a world without forests is as unthinkable as a day without wood. Finding the balance that allows all these apparent contradictions to exist is the challenge for modern thinkers."

—Patrick Moore,
Green Spirit, Trees Are the Answer[5]

117

"WISCONSIN'S FORESTS *are vitally important to the state's environmental and economic health. Forests cover nearly half of our great state and provide an array of benefits that include wildlife habitat, places for outdoor recreation, protection of water quality, biological diversity, jobs in the forest products and tourism sectors, and places in which to live and work. I believe strongly that we must realize these benefits in a manner that ensures both we and future generations of Wisconsin citizens enjoy the same range and extent of benefits associated with our forests."*

—Governor Jim Doyle

Wisconsin forests are in excellent shape to meet the challenges of the future. Wisconsin is growing significantly more wood than is being harvested and there is a growing interest in sustainable forestry practices.

Wisconsin's forests are very important to the state's economy. The forest industry has a significant effect with more than 150,000 jobs in forest products and processing. Forest products and recreation account for 12 percent of the gross state product, and the state leads the nation in paper production. In coming years, Wisconsin will see an increased economic impact of forest-based recreation because of increasing populations and the popularity of these activities.

There also will be greater demand for forest products, making the practice of sustainable forest management even more important.

CHALLENGES

Wisconsin's forests face challenges in the coming years. Issues such as forest certification, exotic and invasive species, fire suppression in the urban-rural interface, and the continued need for private woodland stewardship will challenge professionals and citizens alike. There should be thoughtful consideration of questions such as "What is sustainable forestry?" "Where does the wood that I use in thousands of products each day come from?" and "Why should I care about the well-being of Wisconsin's forests?"

Professional training has already begun for loggers who harvest timber, with the state's first class of master loggers graduating in 2004. The DNR has achieved third-party forest certification for the state forests and is exploring certification for county forests and forestland entered into the Managed Forest Law program.

As more and more people purchase woodlands, the average parcel size is decreasing, bringing the issue of fragmentation to the forefront. While their individual acreages may be small, collectively, private woodland owners own more than 60 percent of Wisconsin's forests. Private landowners should be encouraged to sustainably manage their forestland.

It is important to assist landowners with their management goals and increase the amount of professional assistance and incentives available to them. It is estimated that only 20 percent of private, nonindustrial landowners receive professional assistance prior to having timber harvested from their land. The management of these nonindustrial private lands, with over nine

million acres of forestland, is critical to ensuring the sustainability of Wisconsin's forests.

Perhaps the most significant issue to affect Wisconsin forests in the future will be invasive exotic species. Garlic mustard, honeysuckle, buckthorn, and reed canary grass are already creating havoc in the state's woodlands. In addition, exotic insects including the Asian long-horned beetle and emerald ash borer could have a major impact if they spread to Wisconsin. A healthy forest managed by informed, involved landowners can provide the best defense against these exotic invasive species.

Forests are used for recreation and to provide aesthetic beauty, produce forest products, maintain water quality, and provide wildlife habitat, among many other uses. Not all of these uses are always compatible in the same forest. The debate among people who value the forest for different reasons has grown in recent years. The debate will continue to shape management decisions made in Wisconsin's communities.

With changes in ownership of industrial lands and demographic changes in nonindustrial private land owners, the amount of forested land open for public use is decreasing. This trend will affect public hunting, fishing, and other forms of recreation.

POISED FOR FUTURE SUCCESS

Wisconsin's forests have changed tremendously. Their recovery from the overharvest of timber 100 years ago is nothing less than phenomenal. The future will bring more changes and challenges, but we have learned that forests bend with each new storm of adversity and that they can remain standing strong and ever expanding. As we begin the next 100 years, sustainable forest management will leave a legacy of healthy and vibrant forests for Wisconsin's future generations.

As Paul DeLong, chief state forester, noted, "Future social, economic, and environmental pressures will be different, but we have a duty as a society to find ways to meet our needs without imperiling the ability of forests to meet the needs of future generations. That is the goal of sustainable forestry."

APPENDIX

WISCONSIN FORESTRY HALL OF FAME

The Wisconsin Forestry Hall of Fame was founded by a group of public and private forestry organizations to recognize individuals who have contributed significantly to the practice of forestry in Wisconsin.

Persons may be nominated for induction into the Hall of Fame by member organizations, representatives of member organizations, or individuals through a member organization. Nominees may be professionals or nonprofessionals in the field of forestry or related fields, living or deceased, resident or nonresident. Eligibility is determined by the person's accomplishments and contributions to Wisconsin that have influenced forestry progress in the state. Nominee applications are reviewed on an annual basis by the Hall of Fame committee.

The Hall of Fame exhibit displaying plaques of all inductees is located at the College of Natural Resources building on the UW–Stevens Point campus and is open to the public for viewing free of charge during school hours.

HALL OF FAME INDUCTEES

1984
R. B. Goodman—leader in forest tax reform, rural zoning, and industrial forestry.

E. M. Griffith—first state forester; secured northern lands for forest reserves and recreation.

F. G. Wilson—drafted legislation for county forests and Conservation Act; first UW–Extension forester.

1985
Calvin B. Stott—father of continuous forest inventory in Wisconsin used by major forest landowners.

Melvin Taylor—cofounder of Trees for Tomorrow; advocate for conservation education.

Fred B. Trenk—UW–Extension forester; promoter of school forests; crusader in educational programming.

1986
George Banzhaf—established the first consulting forestry firm to serve industrial and private owners.

Gordon R. Connor—active in timber and logging associations; pioneer in the management of hardwoods.

Stanton W. Meade—pioneer in the paper industry and in sound forest management on Consolidated Papers lands.

1987
D. C. Everest—recognized for his contributions to forestry from 1925 to 1952; chaired 1953 state forestry conference.

Emmett B. Hurst—one of the first industrial foresters; advocate of forest research; 25-year president of Trees For Tomorrow.

Sergius A. Wilde—pioneer in forest soils research; leader in forest nursery and plantation management.

1988
F. George Kilp—industrial forester pioneering reforestation programs; visionary in forest planning.

Neil H. LeMay—chief forest ranger recognized for innovative fire-fighting techniques, equipment, and communications.

Raphael Zon—directed forest research to restore cutover forests; active with political and social leaders.

1989
John A. Beale—professional forester and administrator who developed a state forestry plan.

Earl W. Tinker—first regional forester of the U.S. Forest Service who led in wise and visionary land use.

1990
Nils Folke Becker—leader in the 1920s for public funding for forestry and enactment of the Forest Crop Law.

George Corrigan—devoted his life to improving the lot of the lumberjack and the cause of forestry and conservation.

1991

Ernest Brickner—private forest landowner with a "hands-on" approach to forestry and sound land use.

Richard M. Godman—research forester recognized by his peers for his work in hardwood management for the field forester.

1992

Cornelius L. Harrington—developed early forest policy dealing with recreation; legacy lies in the state's forests and parks.

William A. Sylvester—taught forestry students and led workshops for agriculture teachers; professional forester for 50 years.

1993

H. James Hovind—directed the early restoration of the Marinette County forest; coauthored the 1983 and 1985 Strategic Plan for Wisconsin Forests.

1994

John H. Saemann—managed the Marinette County forest for 33 years; strong proponent of the school forest program.

Stanley W. Welsh—public forester for 41 years; served with distinction in the county and private forestry programs.

1995

William H. Brener—developed the state forest nursery program that produced 900 million tree seedlings in support of the state reforestation program.

Wakelin McNeel—directed the state 4-H forestry and conservation activities for 40 years; best known as "Ranger Mac."

1996

John W. Macon—researcher in forest practices; active in conservation education; served on the Menominee Indian Study committee.

1997

Frank N. Fixmer—industrial forester for the Mosinee paper mills; active in the forest history of Wisconsin; served on various boards, councils, and committees.

1998

George W. Blanchard—state senator from 1924 to 1931 who drafted and secured passage of major forestry legislation that remains the foundation of Wisconsin forestry.

1999

Frederic W. Braun—certified public accountant who shared his love for forestry with the entire state; his business skills made the Wisconsin Woodland Owners Association a successful organization.

Aldo Leopold—nationally recognized forester whose writings and ideas guided foresters and others involved in conservation and the environment.

2000

Milton E. Reinke—state forester with a career with the DNR; strengthened county and private forestry programs and directed the first state strategic forestry plan.

2001

Forest Stearns—professor emeritus and internationally known forest ecologist; provided research on the composition and change of Wisconsin's northern hardwood forests.

2002

No nominees elected.

2003

Increase Allen Lapham—called "the father of forest conservation in Wisconsin"; persuaded the 1867 legislature to create a special forestry commission, which he chaired.

Eugene J. Schmit—president of Wisconsin County Forests Association for 24 years.

2004

Cecil Glenn (Mac) McLaren—Wisconsin's first industrial forester hired in 1927; hosted the 1943 Pulpwood Roundup.

NOTES

Information that does not have a citation has been provided by the Wisconsin Department of Natural Resources.

PROLOGUE

SIDEBARS

1 William G. Rector, *Log Transportation in the Lake States 1840–1918* (Glendale, CA: Arthur H. Clark, 1953).

CHAPTER ONE

1 Forest W. Stearns, "History of the Lake States Forests: Natural and Human Impact," in *Lake States Regional Forest Resources Assessment: Technical Papers*, Gen. Tech. Rep. NG-189, ed. J. Michael Valsievich and Henry H. Webster (St. Paul, MN: U.S. Forest Service, 1997), 8–9; Christopher P. Dunn and Forest Stearns, "Landscape Ecology in Wisconsin," in *John T. Curtis: Fifty Years of Wisconsin Plant Ecology*, ed. J. S. Fralish, R. P. McIntosh, and O. C. Loucks (Madison: The Wisconsin Academy, 1993), 202–3.

2 Robert W. Finley, *Geography of Wisconsin: A Content Outline* (Madison: Regents of the University of Wisconsin System, 1975), 151–7; Filibert Roth, "On the Forestry Conditions of Northern Wisconsin," *Wisconsin Geological and Natural History Survey, Economic Series Bulletin* no. 1 (1898): 10-12.

3 John T. Curtis, *The Vegetation of Wisconsin* (Madison: University of Wisconsin Press, 1959), 461–3.

4 Curtis, *Vegetation of Wisconsin*, 464; Stearns, "History of the Lake States Forests," 10.

5 Mary Dopp, "Geographical Influences in the Development of Wisconsin" ("The Lumber Industry"), *American Geographical Society Bulletin* 45 (1913): 738; Committee on Land Use and Forestry, *Forest Land Use in Wisconsin* (Madison: Wisconsin Executive Office, 1932), 38.

6 George W. Sieber, "Wisconsin Forests," in *Encyclopedia of American Forest and Conservation History*, vol. 2, ed. Richard C. Davis (New York: Macmillan, 1983), 712; Committee on Land Use and Forestry, *Forest Land Use*, 38.

7 James Willard Hurst, "The Institutional Environment of the Logging Era in Wisconsin," in *The Great Lakes Forest: An Environmental and Social History*, ed. Susan L. Flader (Minneapolis: University of Minnesota Press, 1983), 147.

8 Hurst, "Institutional Environment of the Logging Era," 153.

9 Roth, "Forestry Conditions," 16–17.

10 Ray H. Whitbeck, "The Geography and Industries of Wisconsin," Wisconsin Geological and Natural

History Survey, *Educational Bulletin* no. 16 (1913): 20–22; Robert F. Fries, *Empire in Pine: The Story of Lumbering in Wisconsin* 1830–1900, (Sister Bay, Wisc.: Wm. Caxton, 1989), 253; Committee on Land Use and Forestry, *Forest Land Use*, 38.

11 Sieber, "Wisconsin Forests," 711–2; Committee on Land Use and Forestry, *Forest Land Use*, 38; Edward P. Alexander, "Timber!" *Wisconsin Conservation Bulletin* 8 (June 1943): 22.

12 Roth, "Forestry Conditions," 12–13; Dunn and Stearns, "Landscape Ecology," 205.

13 Randall E. Rohe, "Lumbering's Impact on the Landscape of the Wolf River Area of Northeastern Wisconsin" (master's thesis, University of Colorado, 1971), 48.

14 Mitchell and LeMay, "Forest Fires and Forest-Fire Control in Wisconsin," (Madison: Wisconsin State Conservation Commission, 1952); 11–12.

15 Curtis, *Vegetation of Wisconsin*, 469; Raphael Zon, "Forest Conditions in Wisconsin," in *Forestry in Wisconsin* (Menasha, WI: Banta, 1928), 32.

16 Burton L. Dahlberg and Ralph C. Guettinger, *The White-Tailed Deer in Wisconsin* (Madison: Wisconsin Conservation Department, 1956), 14–16.

17 Dahlberg and Guettinger, *White-Tailed Deer in Wisconsin*, 26; Ernest Swift, *A History of Wisconsin Deer* (Madison: Wisconsin Conservation Department, 1946), 14–16; Larsen, *Renewable Resources*, 62; Otis S. Bersing, *A Century of Wisconsin Deer* (Madison: Wisconsin Conservation Department, 1966), 9–10.

18 Curtis, *Vegetation of Wisconsin*, 153–4, 241, 306, 335, 466–8.

19 W. A. Henry, *Northern Wisconsin: A Hand Book for the Homeseeker* (Madison, 1896), 18.

20 Paul W. Glad, *The History of Wisconsin*, vol. 5 (Madison: State Historical Society of Wisconsin, 1990), 204.

21 Committee on Land Use and Forestry, *Forest Land Use*, 29.

22 Committee on Land Use and Forestry, *Forest Land Use*, 29; Glad, *History of Wisconsin*, 104.

23 Arlan Helgeson, *Farms in the Cutover: Agricultural Settlement in Northern Wisconsin* (Madison: State Historical Society of Wisconsin, 1962), 5–7.

24 Roth, "Forestry Conditions," 8, 44; Helgeson, *Farms in the Cutover*, 7.

25 Increase A. Lapham, "The Forest Trees of Wisconsin," *Transactions of the State Agricultural Society* 4 (1854): 195–196.

26 Fries, *Empire in Pine*, 168; James Willard Hurst, *Law*

and Economic Growth: The Legal History of the Lumber Industry in Wisconsin, 1836–1915 (Madison: University of Wisconsin Press, 1984), 59, 68; Edward P. Alexander, "Conservation and Recreation," *Wisconsin Conservation Bulletin* 8 (September 1943): 6.

27 Fred G. Wilson, "History of State Forestry in Wisconsin" (Wisconsin Conservation Department, Madison, 1955, typewritten manuscript), 6.

28 I. A. Lapham, J. G. Knapp, and H. Crocker, *Report of the Disastrous Effects of the Destruction of Forest Trees Now Going On So Rapidly in the State of Wisconsin* (Madison: Atwood and Rublee, 1867), 3.

29 Lapham, Knapp, and Crocker, *Disastrous Effects*, 8–9.

30 Wilson, "History of State Forestry," 6.

31 William W. Morris, "An Early Forest Plantation in Wisconsin," *Wisconsin Magazine of History* 27 (June 1944): 436; "The Wisconsin State Forest Reserve," *Wisconsin Magazine of History* 2 (June 1919): 462–3.

32 Albin R. Santana, "Seventy Years of a Managed Forest," *Wisconsin Conservation Bulletin* 25 (January 1960): 7–8; Carl E. Krog, "Marinette: Biography of a Nineteenth Century Lumbering Town" (PhD dissertation, University of Wisconsin–Madison, 1971), 183–4.

33 Wilson, "History of State Forestry," 6–7.

34 Ibid., 7.

35 Ibid., 8.

36 Harold K. Steen, "Society of American Foresters," in *Encyclopedia of American Forest and Conservation History*, vol. 2, ed. Richard C. Davis (New York: Macmillan, 1983), 613.

37 Wilson, "History of State Forestry," 8; Fred G. Wilson, *E. M. Griffith and the Early Story of Wisconsin Forestry (1903-1915)* (Madison: Wisconsin Department of Natural Resources, 1982), 13.

SIDEBARS

1 Paul Pendowski, "When Peshtigo Burned," *Wisconsin Conservation Bulletin* 26 (July–August 1971): 8–9; Peter Pernin, *The Great Peshtigo Fire: An Eyewitness Account* (Madison: State Historical Society of Wisconsin, 1971), 26; Robert Wells, *Daylight in the Swamp* (Garden City, NY: Doubleday, 1978), 126, 130.

2 Albert M. Swain, "Bottoms Up," *Wisconsin Natural Resources* 3 (January–February 1979): 19.

CHAPTER TWO

1 Donald E. Boles, "Administrative Rule Making In Wisconsin Conservation" (PhD dissertation, University of Wisconsin, 1956), 8, 33; Walter E. Scott, "Conservation History," *Wisconsin Conservation Bulletin* 2 (June 1937): 32.

2 Boles, "Administrative Rule Making," 34; Wilson, E. M. Griffith, 12; Mitchell and LeMay, *Forest Fires*, 17; Vernon Carstensen, *Farms or Forests: Evolution of a State Land Policy for Northern Wisconsin 1850–1932* (Madison: University of Wisconsin, College of Agriculture, 1958), 33–34.

3 Boles, "Administrative Rule Making," 35.

4 Ibid., 34.

5 Wilson, *E. M. Griffith*, 8; Carstensen, *Farms or Forests*, 34; Theodore F. Kouba, *Wisconsin's Amazing Woods: Then and Now* (Madison: Wisconsin House, 1973), 123.

6 Wilson, *E. M. Griffith*, 13; Mitchell and LeMay, *Forest Fires*, 17.

7 Wilson, *E. M. Griffith*, 13; Mitchell and LeMay, *Forest Fires*, 17.

8 Boles, "Administrative Rule Making," 36.

9 Ibid.

10 Wilson, E. M. Griffith, 14–15.

11 Wilson, "History of State Forestry," 10.

12 Kouba, *Amazing Woods*, 124; Mitchell and LeMay, *Forest Fires*, 18.

13 Mitchell and LeMay, *Forest Fires*, 18; Kouba, *Amazing Woods*, 124, 126.

14 Mitchell and LeMay, *Forest Fires*, 18.

15 Ibid.

16 Ibid.

17 Wilson, *E. M. Griffith*, 25.

18 Ibid.

19 Carstensen, *Farms or Forests*, 36; Wilson, *E. M. Griffith*, 30; Charles A. Nelson, *History of the U.S. Forest Products Laboratory (1910–1963)* (Madison: U.S. Forest Service, Forestry Products Laboratory, 1971), 1–2, 38–39, 42–43.

20 Carstensen, *Farms or Forests*, 35–36, 38; Wilson, *E. M. Griffith*, 32.

21 Wilson, "History of State Forestry," 10–11; Kouba, *Amazing Woods*, 126; Mitchell and LeMay, *Forest Fires*, 22.

22 Wilson, "History of State Forestry," 11; Kouba, *Amazing Woods*, 126; Mitchell and LeMay, *Forest Fires*, 22.

23 Wilson, *E. M. Griffith*, 20; Clyde Todd, "Fire in America: A History and Analysis," (1996); 19–20.

24 Wilson, *E. M. Griffith*, 36; Carstensen, *Farms or Forests*, 40.

25 Carstensen, *Farms or Forests*, 43.

26 Boles, "Administrative Rule Making," 44–45.

27 Wilson, "History of State Forestry," 11.

28 Scott, "Conservation History," 36.

29 Mitchell and LeMay, *Forest Fires*, 23.

30 Ibid.

31 Carstensen, *Farms or Forests*, 36; Wilson, *E. M. Griffith*, 38.

32 Carstensen, *Farms or Forests*, 53; Wilson, "History of State Forestry," 5.

33 Robert Gough, *Farming the Cutover* (Lawrence: University of Kansas Press, 1997), 30, 32; Carstensen, *Farms or Forests*, 53.

34 Gough, *Farming the Cutover*, 32–33.

35 Gough, *Farming the Cutover*, 30; Carstensen, *Farms or Forests*, 53, 66.

36 Gough, *Farming the Cutover*, 31, 34.

37 Carstensen, *Farms or Forests*, 55, 57.

38 Mitchell and LeMay, *Forest Fires*, 19; Wilson, "History of State Forestry," 13; Kouba, *Amazing Woods*, 133.

39 Carstensen, *Farms or Forests*, 82.

40 Wilson, "History of State Forestry," 13; Kouba, *Amazing Woods*, 133.

41 Ibid.

SIDEBARS

1 Wilson, *E. M. Griffith*, 27; Carstensen, *Farms or Forests*, 36; Kouba, *Amazing Woods*, 131.

2 Herbert O. Fleischer, "Forest Products Research," in *Encyclopedia of American Forest and Conservation History*, vol. 1, ed. Richard C. Davis (New York: Macmillan, 1983), 123, 232–3; Committee on Land Use and Forestry, *Forest Land Use*, 47; George M. Hunt, "The Forest Products Laboratory," in *Trees: The Yearbook of Agriculture* (Washington, DC: U.S. Department of Agriculture, 1949), 648, 650; Nelson, *History of the U.S. Forest Products Laboratory*, 1, 161.

3 Wilson, *E. M. Griffith*, 42-43; Don Bur, "Star Lake Plantation," *Northbound* 12 (Autumn 1992): 4; Randall Rohe, *Ghosts of the Forests: Vanished Lumber Towns of Wisconsin* (Wisconsin Rapids: The Forest History Association of Wisconsin, 2002), 307–8; "A Billion Trees: The Legend of Fred Wilson" *Wisconsin Natural Resources* 2 (May–June 1978): 12–13.

CHAPTER THREE

1 Carstensen, *Farms or Forests*, 86.

2 Mitchell and LeMay, *Forest Fires*, 23; Erling D. Solberg, *New Laws for New Forests* (Madison: University of Wisconsin Press, 1961), 62.

3 Mitchell and LeMay, *Forest Fires*, 23; Solberg, *New Laws for New Forests*, 63.

4 Carstensen, *Farms or Forests*, 86; Solberg, *New Laws for New Forests*, 62–63; Wilson, "History of State Forestry," 14.

5 Carstensen, *Farms or Forests*, 87; Committee on Land Use and Forestry, *Forest Land Use*, 58.

6 Carstensen, *Farms or Forests*, 87–89.

7 Carstensen, *Farms or Forests*, 91, 94; Glad, *History of Wisconsin*, 206.

8 Carstensen, *Farms or Forests*, 94, Glad, *History of Wisconsin*, 208.

9 Stearns, "History of the Lake States Forests," 15; "Forests and Lands," *Wisconsin Conservation Department Bulletin* 15 (February 1950): 29; Norman J. Schmaltz, "Zon, Raphael (1874–1956)," in *Encyclopedia of American Forest and Conservation History*, vol. 2, ed. Richard C. Davis (New York: Macmillan, 1983), 742.

10 Ralph Swanson, "An Industrial Forest Is Born: Consolidated Papers, Inc.," *Northbound 12* (Autumn 1992): 9; *American Lumberman*, 18 April 1925; *Antigo Journal*, 10 May 1928.

11 *Antigo Journal*, 10 May 1928; *American Lumberman*, 18 April 1925; William A. Holt, *A Wisconsin Lumberman Looks Backward* (Oconto, WI: privately printed, 1948), 74.

12 *New North* (Rhinelander), 2 May 1927; *American Lumberman*, 14 May 1927; *Antigo Journal*, 6 May 1928.

13 Division of Forests and Parks, *Wisconsin State Forests: A Report on Their Origin, Development, Public Usefulness, and Potentialities* (Madison: Wisconsin Conservation Department, 1955), 21.

14 The Natural Resources Committee of State Agencies, *The Natural Resources of Wisconsin* (n.p., 1956), 24; Division of Forests and Parks, *Wisconsin State Forests*, 13.

15 William Sylvester, "School Forests in Wisconsin," in *Where Are We in Wisconsin Forestry Today? Proceedings of the Second Annual Meeting of the Forest History Association of Wisconsin* (Wisconsin Rapids, WI.: The Print Shop, 1978), 7; Ralph R. Widner, ed. *Forests and Forestry in the American States* (Washington, DC: National Association of State Foresters, 1968), 498; Noble Clark, "State Activities in Forestry," in *Forestry in Wisconsin: A New Outlook* (Menasha, WI: George Banta, 1928), 43.

16 Clark, "State Activities in Forestry," 43; "Report to the People of Wisconsin on the State's Natural Resources," *Wisconsin Conservation Bulletin* 15 (February 1950), 62; Fred B. Trenk, "The University of Wisconsin and Wisconsin Forestry," in *Proceedings of the Wisconsin*

Silver Anniversary Forestry Conference (Evansville, WI: Antes Printing Company, 1954), 130.

17 Christine L. Thomas, "Wilhelmine LaBudde: Conservation Advocate, Lady of Letter," *Wisconsin Natural Resources* 18 (February 1994): 20–21.

18 Gough, *Farming the Cutover*, 163.

19 Ibid.

20 Ibid.

21 Glad, *History of Wisconsin*, 208.

22 Glad, *History of Wisconsin*, 208–9; Alexander, "Conservation and Recreation," 8; Carstensen, *Farms or Forests*, 107.

23 Glad, *History of Wisconsin*, 209; Randall E. Rohe, "Goodman: The Company Town That Outlived the Company," *Voyageur: Northeast Wisconsin's Historical Review* 19 (Summer–Fall 2002): 33.

24 Wilson, "History of State Forestry," 18.

25 Gough, *Farming the Cutover*, 169; Carstensen, *Farms or Forests*, 105, 107.

26 Carstensen, *Farms or Forests*, 98.

27 Ibid., 99.

28 Glad, *History of Wisconsin*, 209.

29 Carstensen, *Farms or Forests*, 121–3.

30 Solberg, *New Laws for New Forests*, 70; Committee on Land Use and Forestry, *Forest Land Use*, 41.

31 Glad, *History of Wisconsin*, 208; Carstensen, *Farms or Forests*, 93; Kennell M. Elliott, *History of the Nicolet National Forest 1928–1976* (U.S. Forest Service and Forest History Association of Wisconsin, 1997), 35; *American Lumberman*, 20 July 1929, 59; *American Lumberman*, 20 July 1929, 31 reported the purchase of 30,000 acres in Bayfield County by the federal government.

32 Carstensen, *Farms or Forests*, 93.

33 Ibid.

34 Carstensen, *Farms or Forests*, 99; D. C. Everest, "Wisconsin Forestry's Silver Anniversary: Summary of the Conference," *Wisconsin Conservation Bulletin* 19 (January 1954): 4; M. W. Swenson, "Address of Welcome," in *Proceedings of the Wisconsin Silver Anniversary Forestry Conference* (Evansville, WI: Antes Printing Company, 1954), 3.

35 Carstensen, *Farms or Forests*, 99.

36 Solberg, *New Laws for New Forests*, 86.

37 Ibid.

SIDEBARS

1 Mark E. Bruhy, Angie Teater, Cari VerPlank, and Kim Potarachek, "Velebit: Historical Investigation of an Early 20th Century Croatian Community," in *Nicolet National Forest Heritage Resource Management, Cultural Resource Survey Report Number 7* (Rhinelander, WI:

U.S. Forest Service, 1990), 352, 358–361, 363–6; Gough, *Farming the Cutover*, 135.

2 J. E. Alexander, "Pulpwood Production," in Forestry in Wisconsin (Milwaukee, WI: 1928), 88-90; J. Marshall Bueheler, *The Nekoosa Story* (Port Edwards, WI: Nekoosa Papers, 1987), 102–5.

3 Rohe, "Goodman," 33, 35–36; Allen S. Haukom, "Commission Tours Goodman Forests," *Wisconsin Conservation Bulletin* 17 (January 1952): 23; Alvin E. Nelson and David G. Nelson, *A History of Events of the Wisconsin Society of American Foresters 1919–2000* (Wisconsin Society of American Foresters, 2001), 20.

CHAPTER FOUR

1 Kouba, *Amazing Woods*, 138; Mitchell and LeMay, *Forest Fires*, 29.

2 Stephen J. Pyne, "Firefighting Methods and Equipment," in *Encyclopedia of American Forest and Conservation History*, vol. 1, ed. Richard C. Davis (New York: Macmillan, 1983), 182.

3 William Hulbert, "New Deal Produces a Great Deal: The CCC Legacy," *Timber Producer* (July 1966): 42; Kouba, *Amazing Woods*, 251.

4 W. H. Brener, "Wisconsin Forest Research Program," *Wisconsin Conservation Bulletin* 18 (January 1953): 17.

5 Fred B. Trenk, "Wisconsin's Oldest Shelterbelt," *Wisconsin Conservation Bulletin* 21 (July 1956): 24; Joseph H. Stoeckeler and Ross A. Williams, "Windbreakers and Shelterbelts," in *Trees: The Yearbook of Agriculture* (Washington, DC: U.S. Department of Agriculture, 1949), 193; Wilson, "History of State Forestry," 33.

6 Solberg, *New Laws for New Forests*, 82, 87; Mitchell and LeMay, *Forest Fires*, 31.

7 Mitchell and LeMay, *Forest Fires*, 31.

8 *Antigo Journal*, 31 December 1936; *Forest Republican*, 4 September 1941.

9 "Forests and Land," *Wisconsin Conservation Bulletin* 15 (February 1950): 33.

10 Carstensen, *Farms or Forests*, 125; Gough, *Farming the Cutover*, 181; Charles B. Drewry et al., *From Public Burden to Public Benefit: The Story of Marinette County's Land Program* (Madison: Wisconsin Conservation Department, 1949), 32.

11 Carstensen, *Farms or Forests*, 125; Gough, *Farming the Cutover*, 181.

12 *Forest Republican*, 29 February 1940, 26 April 1945.

13 Chapin Collins, "Industrial Forestry Associations," in *Trees: The Yearbook of Agriculture* (Washington, DC: U.S. Department of Agriculture, 1949), 672; Folke Becker, "Trees for Tomorrow," *Wisconsin Magazine of History* 36 (Autumn 1952): 43; Billie Taylor, "Trees for Tomorrow Camp," *Wisconsin Conservation Bulletin* 26 (January–

February 1961): 30; Ernest Swift, "Trees for Tomorrow: A Study in Grass Roots Conservation," *American Forests*, April 1968, 20–21.

14 Becker, "Trees for Tomorrow," 43; Taylor, "Trees for Tomorrow Camp," 30; Swift, "Trees for Tomorrow," 22.

15 Ernest Swift, "Trees For Tomorrow, Part II: On, Wisconsin," *American Forests*, May 1968, 34.

16 Kouba, *Amazing Woods*, 113.

17 Michael E. Moon, "Smokey Bear," in *Encyclopedia of American Forest and Conservation History*, vol. 2, ed. Richard C. Davis (New York: Macmillan, 1983), 608–9.

SIDEBARS

1 Elliott, *History of the Nicolet National Forest*, 42–43; John A. Salmond, *The Civilian Conservation Corps*, (Durham, NC: Duke University Press, 1967), 30–32, 46, 84,137–8; John Pager, "The Civilian Conservation Corps Program with Emphasis on Wisconsin," in *Proceedings of the Eighth Annual Meeting of the Forest History Association of Wisconsin, Inc.* (Wisconsin Rapids, WI.: The Print Shop, 1984), 11; *Forest Republican*, 29 August 1935; *Antigo Daily Journal*, 31 December 1935; "The CCC Remembers," *Wisconsin Natural Resources* 7 (July–August 1983); *Forest Republican*, 10 June 1937, 16 December 1937; *Oconto County Reporter*, 4 February 1943, 11 February 1943, 29 April 1943, 4 August 1943.

2 Sidney Henderson, "An Experiment in Forest-Farm Resettlement," *Journal of Land and Public Utility Economics* 22 (February 1946): 10–12, 16; Gough, *Farming the Cutover*, 188–90.

3 Moon, "Smokey Bear," 609; Walter W. Lueck, "Fire Prevention via Smokey Bear," *Wisconsin Conservation Bulletin* 22 (May 1957): 26–28.

CHAPTER FIVE

1 John A. Beale, "Opportunity Now: Woodland Management," *Wisconsin Conservation Bulletin* 24 (January 1959): 18.

2 Jeff Martin, "Demonstration Forests," in *Educating the Public in Forestry through 75 Years: Proceedings of the Fifteenth Annual Meeting of the Forest History Association of Wisconsin, Inc.* (Wisconsin Rapids, Wisc.: The Print Shop, 1991), 17.

3 Nelson and Nelson, *Wisconsin Society of American Foresters*, 12–13.

4 Jerry Lapidakis, "History of Private Forestry Assistance," in *Educating the Public in Forestry through 75 Years: Proceedings of the Fifteenth Annual Meeting of the Forest History Association of Wisconsin, Inc.* (Wisconsin Rapids, WI: The Print Shop, 1991), 25.

5 Gordon Cunningham, "Where Are We in Private Forests Today?" *Proceedings of Second Annual Meeting of the Forest History Association of Wisconsin, Inc.* (Wisconsin Rapids, WI: The Print Shop, 1977), 21.

6 Solberg, *New Laws for New Forests*, 112.

7 Lapidakis, "Private Forestry Assistance," 25–26; Beale, "Opportunity Now," 18; Wilson, "History of State Forestry," 33.

8 Wilson, "History of State Forestry," 33; Beale, "Opportunity Now," 18–19.

9 Beale, "Opportunity Now," 18–19.

10 "Forests and Lands," 28; *Forest Republican*, 24 January 1952; "Chequamegon Timber Cut Now at 30,000 Feet," 32.

11 "Chequamegon Timber Cut," 32.

12 Lewis C. French, "Wisconsin's Rebirth of Pine," *American Forests* 57, December 1951, 9, 44.

13 Jay H. Price, "The Federal Forests of Wisconsin," in *Proceedings of the Wisconsin Silver Anniversary Forestry Conference* (Evansville, WI: Antes Printing Company, 1954), 84.

14 Carstensen, *Farms or Forests*, 126; H. J. Hovind and R. B. Hovind, "Multiple Use on County Forests," *Wisconsin Conservation Bulletin* 21 (September 1956): 19, 23.

15 Wilson, "History of State Forestry," 35; Division of Forests and Parks, *Wisconsin State Forests*, 4, 9.

16 Wilson, "History of State Forestry," 36.

17 Kouba, *Amazing Woods*, 139; Beale, "Opportunity Now," 19.

18 *Shawano Evening Leader*, 11 April 1949; *Milwaukee Journal*, 14 August 1955; Jim Fazio, "Wisconsin Landmark Becomes Most Modern Mill," *Northern Logger and Timber Processor* (April 1969): 52–53; "Tigerton Lumber Company: 75 Years 1887–1962" (1962, unpublished manuscript), 5–6; John Calkins, "Tigerton Lumberman Invested in Faith, Future Forests," *Timber Producers Bulletin*, (May 1953) 17–18; *Milwaukee Journal*, 14 August 1955; *Post Crescent*, 5 March 1997.

19 "Forests and Land," 33; Hardy L. Shirley, "Large Private Holdings in the North," in *Trees: The Yearbook of Agriculture* (Washington, DC: U.S. Department of Agriculture, 1949), 272; Wilson, "History of State Forestry," 31; Gil Zieman, "Symbol of Good Forestry," *Wisconsin Conservation Bulletin* 26 (July–August 1961): 10.

20 F. G. Kilp, "Industrial Forestry in Wisconsin," *Wisconsin Conservation Bulletin* 19 (March 1954): 18–19.

21 E. B. Hurst, "Industrial Forests of Wisconsin," *Wisconsin Conservation Bulletin* 25 (May 1960): 31.

22 Collins, "Industrial Forestry Associations," 672.

23 Taylor, "Trees for Tomorrow Camp," 30.

24 George Banzhaf & Company, "History," www.GbandCo.com/.

25 "Forests and Land," 28.

26 Everest, "Wisconsin Forestry's Silver Anniversary," 3.

27 Ibid.

28 Ibid., 4.

29 Ibid., 5–7.

30 Forest Stearns and Cliff Germain, "Natural Areas Preservation Council: A Brief History and Record of Activity 1951–1991," *Wisconsin Endangered Resources Report* 77 (Madison: Wisconsin Department of Natural Resources, December 1991), i; Evelyn Howell and Forest Stearns, "The Preservation, Management, and Restoration of Wisconsin Plant Communities: The Influence of John Curtis and His Students," in *John T. Curtis: Fifty Years of Wisconsin Plant Ecology*, ed. J. S. Fralish, R. P. McIntosh, and O. C. Loucks (Madison: The Wisconsin Academy, 1993), 58; Clifford E. Germain, William E. Tans, and Robert H. Read, "Wisconsin Scientific Areas 1977: Preserving Native Diversity," *Department of Natural Resources, Technical Bulletin* No. 102 (Wisconsin Department of Natural Resources, 1977), 20.

31 Howell and Stearns, "Preservation, Management, and Restoration," 58; Stearns and Germain, "Natural Areas Preservation Council," 1–2.

32 Cathy Harrington, ed., *The Places We Save: A Guide to The Nature Conservancy's Preserves in Wisconsin* (Minocqua, WI: Northwood Press, 1977), 12, 14, 107.

33 Solberg, *New Laws for New Forests*, 382–3.

SIDEBARS

1 F. B. Trenk and H. F. Scholz, "The Wausaukee Timber Harvest Forest," *Wisconsin Conservation Bulletin* 25 (March 1960): 30–31.

2 Henry Clepper, *Professional Forestry in the United States* (Baltimore, Md.: Johns Hopkins University Press, 1971), 262–3.

CHAPTER SIX

1 Gaylord Nelson, "Beyond Earth Day: Fulfilling the Promise," (Madison: University of Wisconsin Press, 2002).

2 Michael F. Sohasky, *Wisconsin County Forests: Conflict over Indian Treaty Rights* (Friendship, WI: New Past Press, 1994).

CHAPTER SEVEN

1 The Society of American Foresters, *So You Want to Be in Forestry*; Wisconsin Society of American Foresters, *Growing Forests for Our Future* (November 30, 2000).

2 *Certified Woods: Ingraining Sustainable Forestry* (Wisconsin Department of Natural Resources, 2002).

3 Duncan Harkin

4 Marshall Pecore

5 Patrick Moore, "Green Spirit, Trees Are the Answer," (Greenspirit Enterprises, 2000).

PHOTO CREDITS

WHS—WISCONSIN HISTORICAL SOCIETY
WDNR—WISCONSIN DEPARTMENT OF NATURAL RESOURCES

COVER ... WDNR
iv .... Robert Queen/WDNR
vi .... WDNR
viii .... Robert Queen/WDNR
x .... WDNR
2–3 .... WDNR
4 .... WDNR
6 .... WHS Whi (w6) 11643
7 .... WHS Whi (x3) 35052
8 .... WHS Whi (x3) 37710
10 .... WHS 1859
11 .... WHS Whi (x3) 26186
12 .... Top: Vogeler; Bottom: *The Geography & Industries of Wisconsin* by Ray H. Whitbeck
13 .... Courtesy Randall Rohe
14 .... Left: WHS 10565; Right: WHS 2216
15 .... Left: UW-Madison Archives; Right: WHS 2118
16 .... *Farming the Cutover* by Robert Gough
17 .... UW-Madison Archives
18 .... *Farms or Forests: Evolution of a State Land Policy for Northern Wisconsin 1850-1932* by Vernon Carstensen
19 .... Left: DNR 16669; Right: DNR 13221
22 .... WDNR 13691
25 .... WDNR
28 .... Courtesy Randall Rohe
29 .... Forest Products Laboratory
30 .... Top: WDNR 15894; Bottom: WDNR 15893
31 .... WDNR 1569
32 .... Left: DNR 8943; Right: DNR 16722
34 .... WDNR 19887
35 .... UW–Madison Archives
38 .... UW–Madison Archives
40 .... WHS Whi (x3) 31674
41 .... WHS Whi (x3) 36966
42 .... WHS Whi (W63) 11799
45 .... WDNR 3590
46 .... Left: WDNR 15379; Right: WHS 2290
47 .... Courtesy Randall Rohe
50 .... WHS PH 3789
51 .... WHS 6796
52 .... WDNR 1919
54 .... WHS PH 3789
55 .... WDNR 1135
56 .... Top: WDNR 10964; Bottom: WDNR 4368

57 .... WDNR 16479
58 .... Drummond Historical Society
61 .... WHS (x3) 51513
62 .... WDNR 5615
65 .... WDNR 16786
66 .... WDNR 14768
68 .... WDNR 13665
69 .... WDNR 11896
71 .... WDNR 13766
74 .... WDNR 2813
75 .... Clockwise from top left: WDNR 2382, WDNR 13989, WDNR, WDNR
76 .... WDNR 12371
79 .... Gaylord Nelson
80 .... WDNR
81 .... Waukesha County Tourism Initiative
82 .... Thomas A. Meyer/WDNR
83 .... WDNR
84 .... Thomas A. Meyer/WDNR
85 .... UW–Stevens Point News Services
86 .... Michael Forster Rothbart/UW–Madison University Communications
90 .... WDNR
92 .... Nancy C. Bozek/WWOA
96 .... JMAR FOTO-WERKS/WDNR
98 .... WDNR
99 .... WDNR
100 .... WDNR
102 .... WDNR
103 .... WDNR
105 .... U.S. Forest Service/Chequamegon–Nicolet National Forest
106 .... Larry Mancl/Tri-County School District
107 .... WDNR
109 .... Wisconsin Department of Tourism
110 .... Robert Queen/WDNR
111 .... WDNR
113 .... WDNR
114 .... WDNR
115 .... WDNR
116 .... WDNR
118 .... Trails Media Group Inc.
121 .... Trails Media Group Inc.
Photos in the color insert were provided by WDNR unless otherwise noted.